1000 Days on the River Kwai

1000 Days on the River Kwai

The Secret Diary of a British Camp Commandant

Colonel Cary Owtram OBE

Pen & Sword
MILITARY

First published in Great Britain in 2017 by
Pen & Sword Military
an imprint of
Pen & Sword Books Ltd
47 Church Street
Barnsley
South Yorkshire
S70 2AS

ISBN 978 1 47389 780 9

A CIP catalogue record for this book is
available from the British Library.

Printed and bound in England
By CPI Group (UK) Ltd, Croydon, CR0 4YY

Pen & Sword Books Ltd incorporates the Imprints of Pen & Sword Books
Archaeology, Atlas, Aviation, Battleground, Discovery, Family History, History,
Maritime, Military, Naval, Politics, Railways, Select, Transport, True Crime,
Fiction, Frontline Books, Leo Cooper, Praetorian Press, Seaforth Publishing,
Wharncliffe and White Owl.

For a complete list of Pen & Sword titles please contact
PEN & SWORD BOOKS LIMITED
47 Church Street, Barnsley, South Yorkshire, S70 2AS, England
E-mail: enquiries@pen-and-sword.co.uk
Website: www.pen-and-sword.co.uk

Their bodies are buried in peace, but their name
liveth for evermore.

Ecclesiasticus 44:14

Contents

Foreword

This book, based on his secretly kept wartime diaries, was written by Colonel Cary Owtram a few years after his return from more than three years' captivity in Thailand as a prisoner of war of the Japanese. At the time he failed to find a publisher, and the manuscript was given to the Imperial War Museum along with the original diaries. Now, more than sixty years later, it is being published, with the addition of a postscript in which his daughters Patricia Davies and Jean Argles add their memories of the effect on the family of his imprisonment and eventual release.

The text is exactly as it was written in 1953, with one exception. It will be clear to the reader that the Author returned from the war with an understandably deep hatred of the Japanese, and this was reflected in some of his language. Certain terms that were commonplace in the aftermath of the war (for example, referring to the Japanese as 'Nips') are now unacceptable, and such references have been toned down, although hopefully without obscuring the strength of the author's feelings.

Preface

When I returned home in October 1945, after three and a half years as a prisoner of war of the Japanese, I brought with me a diary which I had written up regularly for a greater part of the time, as well as a number of records of matters of more particular importance or interest in connection with our existence. As the Japanese searches for such things became increasingly thorough, I buried them in a sealed bottle in a British soldier's grave, but was able to retrieve them at the end of hostilities.

Friends and relations have urged me from time to time to write an account of our experiences as PoWs and so, having records to refer to where owing to the passage of time memory might have failed me, I have written the story of our existence – for one can hardly call it anything else – as seen from a rather different viewpoint to that of other published accounts.

British Camp Commandant of the largest PoW camp in Siam (Thailand) for approximately two years, I probably had a wider knowledge of what was going on in all directions than some of those whose spheres of activity were necessarily more limited so far as administration was concerned.

This book is written as a tribute to the unconquerable spirit of all British, Australian, American and Dutch PoWs in Siam, compelled by brute force to perform a superhuman task far beyond the limits of normal human endurance, but who, by their faith in God, loyalty to each other and sheer guts, were given strength to survive. It is dedicated to the memory of many thousands more whose bodies are buried in Siam and Malaya (Malaysia).

They lie amid the peace and beauty of a picturesque land, but their memory lives forever with us who survived.

The names I have used throughout are real, and I trust that their owners will forgive me for taking this liberty.

I am grateful to several people for the production of this book. To my wife and family for encouragement and help during the time I was writing it; to Mrs Vera Currier for many hours of typing and correction; and to John F. Leeming, himself an author and a friend of long standing, for a great deal of useful advice in putting it into shape.

Cary Owtram
December 1953

Chapter 1

Outward Bound

On a murky, wet Sunday in September 1941, the 137th Field Regiment, in which I was then serving as Second in Command, embarked at Liverpool in SS *Dominion Monarch*. That evening, we nosed our way down the Mersey to join a large convoy collecting in the Irish Sea and consisting of about twenty liners and cargo boats, with an escort of cruisers and destroyers.

This was the beginning of an active share in the war, for which we had been training for two years, and everyone was, rather naturally, keyed up with a sense of excitement and anticipation, particularly as the majority of us had little idea of our ultimate destination. All we knew was that a 'tropical' country was indicated by the kit we had drawn.

Passing slowly down the Mersey and over the bar, we anchored for the night while the rest of the convoy formed up. Next morning, we moved out into the Irish Sea, and as the coastline faded in the distance, the last bit of England we were to see for many a long day was the top of Blackpool Tower disappearing in the haze, a reminder of the early days of the war when many of us had spent the first six months there – the birthplace of the regiment.

Our course took us almost to the North American coast and then south in a wide sweep back to Freetown, Sierra Leone, where we spent two sweltering days gazing from the ship at the sinister-looking coast, clad with Rackham-like trees and thick, tropical jungle. From there we proceeded to Cape Town, where the memory of the welcome we received will remain with us always. The hospitality showered upon us was positively embarrassing, and our four-day stay was all too short.

From Cape Town we sailed across the Indian Ocean, touching for a few hours at Colombo, where we picked up the ill-fated *Repulse* as part of our escort; and on 29 November we drew alongside the quay in Keppel Harbour at Singapore, our final destination.

After more than eight weeks at sea with little opportunity for exercise, the entire regiment of seventeen hundred excited men hurled themselves at the job of unloading our baggage on to the quayside, to the accompaniment of rattling derrick chains and screaming Chinese dock workers. After the enforced idleness of the sea voyage, sweat poured off us as we heaved and pushed the heavy baggage beneath the blazing heat of a tropical sun until everything was out of the ship.

The same evening, most of the regiment moved by train to a little village called Kajang, just south of Kuala Lumpur, some 250 miles north of Singapore, leaving the drivers and a fatigue party behind to unload our guns, vehicles and stores, which arrived on a slower ship a day or two later.

At Kajang we had a few days in which to begin getting ourselves acclimatized to the tropics. Two months at sea, although it had given us a suntan, had left us all a bit soft.

Events moved quickly after this. On the same day that the party we had left behind started on their 250-mile drive with the guns and trucks, the Japanese bombed Singapore and landed on the north-east coast of Malaya, near Khota Bahru.

The regiment was attached to the 23rd Indian Corps, and the Corps Commander ordered the regiment to proceed, as soon as we had got our guns and equipment, to the north of Malaya.

The gun party arrived in Kajang about dusk on the Sunday evening, and it was a truly astonishing sight to see the entire regiment fall upon guns and trucks like a swarm of ants and, with fires burning all night to provide boiling water, wash the grease and dust off them, oil and service them, sort out the thousand and one bits of equipment and pack them into their appointed trucks.

Working all night and the next morning, we had two batteries ready to move off at 1.00 pm, which was the appointed time for our move. The third battery was to follow by rail the next day.

We did the long trip north in three hops. The first night we arrived at Ipoh about midnight and left again at daybreak, passing through the much more beautiful country of Perak, with its rocky outcrops of white limestone gleaming in the bright sun and set amid the deep green of the jungle splashed with paler greens and yellows.

On again through miles of rubber plantations, with their row upon row of grey trunks; through native villages full of colourfully dressed Tamils waving and raising their fists with thumbs up in a signal of 'good luck' as we passed by in a long column of guns, trucks and bren-carriers. Children by the score waved and cheered the British troops who were to drive the invader back from Malaya so easily. Little did we or they know how soon they would see us again, fighting tenaciously and contesting every mile as we withdrew down the peninsula.

The second day's driving brought us that evening to Sungel Patani, a large camp in the rubber with a most depressing atmosphere under its canopy of green leaves. It is an acknowledged fact that rubber is depressing. Whether it is the monotony of line upon line of grey trunks around one in every direction and the dim twilight under the canopy of green overhead, or whether it is the carbon dioxide which the trees give off, I don't know; but the fact remains that all troops did find these camps in the rubber plantations had a depressing effect.

That night, I arranged to meet our other battery on its arrival at the station. It was due about midnight but did not arrive until 7.00 am, so I got no sleep again after having had only three hours the previous night and little more the night before.

That day was spent in preparing for the final stage, which was to bring us into our first battle position. The Colonel and the three Battery Commanders went forward during the day to reconnoitre positions, and I was left to bring the regiment up after dark. At six o'clock that evening we moved off, the long column occupying several miles. Rain fell in torrents as we drove with sidelights only along unknown roads, following the route on my map by the aid of a shaded electric torch. About midnight we arrived at Tanjong Pau, some five miles north of Alor Star, where we were met by the Colonel and his party. Batteries were taken over by their Battery Commanders and Regimental Headquarters were piloted into a camp in the ubiquitous rubber. After posting sentries and having something to eat we got a short spell of sleep, either in our trucks or in huts, and awoke at dawn to the sound of firing a mile or so to our front.

At 8.00 am that day, 12 December 1941, the 350th Battery opened up with the first rounds the regiment had fired in real warfare, their target a bridge which the Japanese were crossing.

The Japanese attack pressed forward all along the front in this sector, and by the afternoon all troops were ordered to retire along the Alor Star road to a village some ten miles back. This was easier said than done, as there was only one road and it was a mass of transport and guns withdrawing, while other vehicles were bringing up ammunition or coming up empty for loads of supplies or to transport the infantry back. If the Japanese had used planes at this stage they could have created utter chaos, but they didn't. Later on, they realized the possibilities open to them and put their planes to good effect.

We got back – at least, most of us did – to the village, which was down a side road, and spent nearly twenty-four hours there waiting for orders, then had to 'up sticks' in the middle of the night down a track through the rubber to Gurun. This was a nightmare drive, with guns and vehicles frequently bogged in the deep ruts. We arrived at Gurun in the small hours of the morning to find it impossible to move further as the road was completely blocked by a mass of vehicles heading south.

Having got out of my truck to try and sort out the jam, I remember an irate brigadier putting his head out of the Utility Truck and cursing me up and down for not doing anything. As I had been directing traffic and cursing Indian drivers in fluent English for half an hour with – as I thought – some measure of success, I felt that this accusation was uncalled-for. Eventually we got on the move, and Regimental Headquarters, for which I was responsible, took possession of a vacated camp in the rubber. About 5.00 pm, after seeing the troops were provided for, I decided to have a couple of hours sleep. I lay down on a *charpoy* (Indian-style bed) with my pack for a pillow, and the next thing I was conscious of was George Holme, the Colonel of the Regiment, telling me it was seven o'clock the next morning. We had both endured about five days and nights with practically no sleep, so perhaps it was not surprising.

From now onwards we seldom spent more than forty-eight hours in one place, but withdrew steadily down the peninsula. More than once the regiment was the last of our troops to withdraw, holding various river bridges while the infantry were pulled back, tired and decimated, to form another line of defence. Poor fellows, they had a tough time, particularly the Argyll & Sutherland Highlanders, the Leicesters and the Surreys. We did at least move on wheels and when we went into action we did stay put for a time, but they got no rest at all.

One day, Captain Freddie Thompson of the Leicesters turned up in our lines with a handful of men. They had been cut off further north and had made their way over a shoulder of Kedah Peak – the highest mountain in Malaya – to the coast and then down to the mouth of the Muda River by *sampan* (Malayan canoe). We kept them with us for several days and gave them food and new clothes and kit.

There was a funny incident on our way south at Bagan Serai – at least it was funny for some, though death to others. We had drawn up under the cover of some trees along the right-hand side of the road for a bit of food and rest and were about to move off, when four Japanese bombers flew over. I told my driver not to move until they had gone and was about to tell him to start, which was the signal for the whole column to move, when back they came over some big tin-roofed rice godowns (warehouses) just across the road into which a lot of Tamils had run to cover. The planes, flying low, dropped a stick of bombs right across the godowns. Freddie Thompson was in the back of my Utility Truck, and like one man he and my driver flung open both the offside doors and disappeared with a splash into the waters of a deep, dirty ditch. I was left sitting in the car to watch the bombs crash through the warehouse roofs some fifty yards away. The casualties inside must have been heavy, but luckily none of us in the column were hit, though a few small bits of debris hit my car and some of our trucks. Presently, two dripping figures emerged from the ditch and re-entered the car, and we left in a hurry before anything worse could befall us.

We usually spent the nights in or under our vehicles, but as we moved south we began to find empty houses belonging to planters and took possession of these for the time being. Most of them had been left full of furniture and silver; in fact, they contained everything except their owners and what they could take away in their cars. As we vacated them, they were ransacked by masses of Tamils, who doubtless stripped them bare. It seemed an awful shame, but we couldn't do anything about it. At some of these bungalows the Chinese 'boys' had stayed to look after their masters' property and used to receive us as though we were guests, putting on their white coats, cooking for us and helping us in our purchases from local shops.

At one place to which I went ahead to reconnoitre before a withdrawal I found the manager of the plantation packing up his belongings preparatory to leaving the place. He was most helpful, insisting on us using his bungalow and all the buildings around. He was in the local defence force and already detailed for duty as a private soldier, but when he asked if we would have him as a liaison officer, it seemed like an excellent idea. The Colonel was a bit dubious, although he finally acquiesced, so Jim Stoker joined us and we gave him a couple of 'pips'. He was a great asset for the short time he was with us as he could talk Tamil and Malay and knew the country well.

Christmas Eve found Regimental Headquarters at a bungalow appositely named 'Peacehaven', about 5 miles north of Ipoh. My job as second in command was largely administrative, and in this capacity I went shopping in the town, though it was being evacuated at the time. I bought quite a good selection of Christmas fare, including some tinned plum pudding. The next day, I thought I would see if I could get enough to make Christmas dinner for all the troops, so returned to the shop where I had been successful before. It was an English store, but the staff had left that day as Ipoh was being evacuated, and I found it barred and shuttered. While I was walking from door to door, a Chinese who had served me the day before, came up and said, 'You come with me', led me up the fire-escape at the back, seized an axe and burst open a door leading into a stock room, then said, 'Evellybody gone – please help yourself.' I was rather shaken by this generosity with somebody else's property but, as he pointed out, if I didn't take it the Japanese would; so with my conscience somewhat salved I descended to the truck and got my driver to help. We filled the Utility with everything one usually associates with Christmas – even to half a dozen bottles of 'Moet' – and returned to Regimental Headquarters triumphant. On the way I called at one of the Battery HQs and told them, and they went hot-foot to the shop with a 3-tonner. The following day, when I passed again, the place had been completely ransacked by hordes of natives.

Our air force in Malaya by this time had ceased to exist in the battle area, with the exception of a small convoy of six Brewster Buffaloes – single-engined fighters – which were based on the Ipoh aerodrome. Their intrepid pilots faced a hopeless task, with almost certain death before them. Completely outmatched in speed, armament and numbers by the Japanese 'Navy O' fighters and twin-engined bombers, they did what they could to harass the advancing enemy. The last time I saw them in the air was on one of the expeditions to Ipoh which I have just mentioned. I had occasion to go to the railway station about something or other and as I got out of my truck, hearing the sound of aero engines, I looked up and noted with satisfaction they were 'ours'. Ten minutes later, having driven to the racecourse buildings on another mission, I got out of the truck, hearing what I thought were the Buffaloes again, and smiled with a feeling of superiority at someone about 50yds away who was gesticulating wildly and pointing up in the air above me, as though the planes over my head were 'Jap' planes. I walked casually on and, looking up to watch them pass over my head, was a bit startled to see six Japanese fighters just above me. They dived straight down on to the racecourse where the Buffaloes had landed two minutes earlier and shot them up as they sat there defenceless.

After Ipoh we withdrew through the more hilly and picturesque country to the south, down through Bidor, Tapar and Sungkair; our next stop was at Bikam Rubber Estate. From here we sent one Battery down the road to the west to try and repel a seaborne landing on the coast at Teluk Anson. The Artillery Brigadier wanted a telephone wire laying across the base of a triangle about 8 miles long, which would otherwise have meant a line of some 20 miles round, for which we hadn't enough wire. Our signal section had one try at it and said it was impossible as it meant laying cable through 6 miles of virgin jungle. However, the Brigadier said it was to be done somehow, so I offered to take a party and have a shot at it. I collected Jim Stoker, our planter friend, and some of the Signal section and started off. The first two miles were easy enough as there was a path to a *kampong* (Malay village). After that there wasn't any path, but Jim spoke to some natives who said there had been a track and we might still find traces of it. That's all we did find, but with the aid of a compass we kept our direction, and after about four hours of hacking creepers and undergrowth with the *parangs* (long-bladed choppers), swimming one or two black and forbidding-looking streams and blazing a trail as we went, we eventually came to cultivated land again, more or less where we intended to arrive.

As I wanted to return to Regimental Headquarters as soon as possible, I went off in one of the Battery vehicles, expecting to be able to ring up the Battery by the time I got back. However, there was no reply and nothing happened for some time; then we heard that two signallers, who had returned for more wire, appeared to have lost themselves in the jungle, as the rest of the party had got through but couldn't locate these fellows. So I asked if any of the subalterns at RHQ would like a walk through the jungle, and Louis Baume volunteered; he and I duly set off in the dark with a storm lantern to repeat the trip. Of course it wasn't so bad the second time as we had the trail to follow and the telephone cable whenever we could spot it – which wasn't often – but it was an eerie feeling in dense blackness in a country which we knew supported a number of the more vicious jungle animals; you must remember, too, that we had only been in the country about a month and hadn't had time to learn much about it. All the same, it was quite good fun and we got through again, only to find the two missing signallers hadn't lost themselves; we had miscalculated the time it would take them to do the double journey, and they had got through about two hours early. I was ready for bed all right that night.

I nearly put my car in the ditch the next day: I was driving happily along and heard noises on the right; looking up, I saw a Japanese fighter about 50yds away, the pilot looking out and grinning at me. He couldn't shoot at me, I suppose, as he couldn't turn the direction of his guns, so he left me alone and had a few shots at a wretched dispatch rider on his motorbike half a mile ahead, fortunately without doing him any harm.

We stayed about a week in this HQ. While we were there, the civilian authorities, corresponding to our Home Guard, wanted to set fire to the big rubber factory and store sheds; but as we were occupying them and all our vehicles were parked under the rubber trees around about, we took a poor view of this. Fires always attracted Japanese planes to the scene to see what was going on.

Eventually, I undertook to set fire to them when we left and with three matches I started a huge holocaust which destroyed probably about £80,000 worth of sheets of crepe rubber, bales and machinery. It seemed like committing arson, but it had to be done. It is a pity more wasn't destroyed, as the Japs got a lot of free rubber eventually.

Chapter 2

Slim River

Our next move brought us down to the banks of the Slim River, which was the scene of disaster for the Regiment and other units. Advanced Headquarters was some miles nearer the line, and there the Commanding Officer and the Adjutant remained while I looked after the main party.

On the morning of 7 January, just after daylight, while I was shaving, heavy firing broke out about 2 miles away in the direction of the main road running south, just about where 349 and 501 Batteries were 'resting' in the rubber. I threw on some clothes and jumped on a motorbike to try and find out what was happening. As we were about 10 miles behind the supposed line I didn't know what could be going on, but thought it might be ammunition blowing up. Just before I reached the main road I was stopped and told not to go any further as about eighteen Japanese tanks had broken through and had passed this point. This accounted for the firing, of course, but was an unpleasant surprise as we had been told (a) that the Japanese weren't using tanks, and (b) they couldn't break through if they tried. It seemed stupid to proceed on a bike after this information so I went back and ordered Regimental Headquarters to get mobile and prepare to move or fight – whichever necessity arose first. Then I returned to the road, intending to go down through the rubber on foot to see what had happened to our batteries. As I was finding out the latest information from an officer near the corner, along came my Commanding Officer, George Holme, also on a motorbike, and alone.

He wanted to know what had happened, and when I told him he expressed his intention of riding down to the battery 'hides'. We had a long argument, during which I told him it wasn't his job but that I would go – on my feet. George insisted on going – on his bike – and ordered me to go back. I let him start and then followed, but he soon found I was following and stopped. He got quite angry and said, 'I've given you an order – kindly obey it.' I was older than he was and we were the best of friends, but he was the CO giving an order to his junior, and reluctantly I obeyed it. Not to have done so, even though he was taking a foolhardy and uncalled-for risk, would have been a serious breach of discipline and would have broken the relationship in which we both served. Many times since I have wondered whether I ought to have refused to obey the order. We know what happened: he rode down the road and met a Jap tank on a corner, as I had warned him would be the case. An officer of another regiment was on the road behind him and saw him shot as he turned the bend.

So died a very brave and able soldier.

At the time, of course, we were unaware of all this, and I returned to my HQ and found them ready for an immediate move.

By this time, all sorts of bits and pieces of units were congregating down our side road, finding they could get no further, and Indian infantry started pouring through, many of them in a state of panic, dropping rifles and bren guns as they ran.

I would like to emphasize the point that nearly all these men were very young soldiers who had only been in the Indian Army a matter of weeks, and the constant withdrawals and infiltrating tactics of the Japs had reduced their morale to a low ebb. It did not by any means apply to the Indian troops as a whole; there were a number of Indian Regiments who fought tenaciously and magnificently throughout the campaign and for whom no praise is too high, but the peculiar type of warfare in which we were engaged strained the nerves of even the best trained troops. I had several instances that day among my own men of loss of morale necessitating firm handling.

I met two brigadiers during the morning and placed myself under their orders; we had frequent discussions as to our procedure as the day wore on. Ultimately it was decided to move at 4 o'clock, withdrawing on foot to the railway bridge over the Slim River behind us with the intention of crossing and walking along the line to Tanjong Malim, some 17 miles south. By the time we moved, the Japs were fairly close. It took a long time getting every-one over the bridge, which had been blown up the day before by our own Engineers, as there were about 2,000 men to get across, one at a time. The river was only about 50yds wide here, so seeing what a slow job it was going to be, I called out to the men near me, 'Anyone who can swim, follow me', jumped in and swam across. A lot followed me and that speeded things up, but it is hard work swimming with a rifle and a belt of ammunition as well as one's pack, haversack and as much other equipment as one could carry; fortunately, it only proved necessary to swim for about 25 yards, but that was far enough. A lot of men let their rifles go halfway and others lost their kit in the water, but there were no casualties.

On the other side I joined the two brigadiers who were watching the troops cross to comparative safety. Spasmodic rifle shots sent bullets pinging past us, but the Japs firing them were rotten shots and hit no one.

When everyone in the party was over, one of the brigadiers asked me to arrange for a small party to stay behind and do what we could to discourage the Japs from crossing the bridge, while he led the party a mile down the track and halted them so that they could be sorted out. I asked for five volunteers and immediately got them from my own Regiment. Our little party included my RSM Verrel and my driver Merrifield – grand fellows to have in any trouble – and three others.

We lay on the embankment for about two hours, fervently hoping the Japs wouldn't try to cross the river up- or downstream and cut us off, because they could do so anywhere without us seeing them. Fortunately, they evidently thought they had gone far enough for one day and we saw no one before dusk, when – rather thankfully – we considered our role completed and walked back to join the main body. Then began a nightmare march through the night. Perhaps 'march' is hardly the right word; those of us who had swum the River Slim were now to regret it. Our boots were full of sand and everything we were wearing and carrying was soaked through and weighed about three times as much as it would have done dry. The night was pitch black and our line was the sleepered single-line track. In places there was a track to one side of it, but more often one had to step either on each sleeper or on the loose ballast between them. The sleepers seemed to have been laid with no definite and fixed space between them just to make it more uncomfortable.

Frequently there were bridges over streams of varying width, and here one had to step from sleeper to sleeper or one would fall through. My recollections of the last few miles are rather hazy but I remember a young Argyll coming along and asking me in a dazed voice, 'Have you seen the Colonel's batman? I must find him.' He then sat down and fell asleep beside me. As we got word to move again, I shook him and told him we'd got to move on;

he got up without a word and strode off down the line like an automaton. I think we stopped about every mile for the last 3 or 4 miles, but eventually we came to Tanjong Malim about 2.00 am and I seem to remember it being moonlight. I sat down in the road and an 'Aussie' from a truck parked nearby came across and said, 'Like a cup of tea?' I shall never forget that tea, it was the best tea I ever drank and they gave me two big mugs full and some to several others with me.

About 4.00 am Australian drivers took us down to Kuala Lumpur. The members of my own Regiment who had arrived in Tanjong Malim early on found a small camp, which our QM had annexed, and ultimately I contacted them there.

That day and the next were spent in re-equipping ourselves as far as possible, as we had lost all our kit at Slim River.

The Jap tanks which had caused the débacle were ultimately stopped by a shot from one of the 4.5 Hows [howitzers] of 155 Field Regiment, which stopped the first tank on a bridge and held up the others behind.

I received orders to report to the CRA at the Batu Caves, a village on the outskirts of KL to which we had withdrawn the following day. He told me about the report he had received regarding G. Holme's death and then told me that I was appointed to command what was left of the Regiment.

He said it had been decided to keep 350 Battery, which had withdrawn just ahead of the Jap tanks and so had remained intact, and to attach it to 155 Field, while I was to take what was left of the other two Batteries down to Singapore with the object of re-equipping one Battery and RHQ.

When the tanks came through on the morning of the 7th, they took 349 and 501 unawares and proceeded to shoot them up from the road. Both Batteries endeavoured to man and bring several guns into action as the tanks moved on down the road. The Batteries then moved two guns each on to the road facing up and down, but as they were doing so another lot of tanks came along. Two of the guns got a round off before being hit themselves and put out of action. The tanks then shot up whatever they could see and moved on again.

Infantry – mostly the same young Indian troops whom I have mentioned before – began to trickle back saying the Japanese had broken through and were on their heels. This, of course, was a gross exaggeration, but no doubt the spirit of panic had grown among them with the sound of firing in their rear, something which is always disconcerting.

The fact remains that this Japanese strategy had probably a greater success than even they could have hoped.

For lack of information of the true facts, our two Batteries decided that it would be easier to 'blow' the remaining guns and destroy any vehicles which were still intact, and having done so, they set off in parties through the jungle in the direction of Tanjong Malim.

Some parties got through and linked up with my party, but a large number got lost in the jungle and were unable to keep ahead of the Japs. They were either taken prisoner, killed or died of exhaustion in the jungle. A sad end to the Regiment's career. About forty have never been accounted for and never will be now.

Whether they could have done any better is a moot point; if they had disregarded the information that Jap infantry were almost upon them, and had kept their guns intact, they would have been overrun later the same day and the Japs would have captured some valuable armament. No more Jap tanks came forward, so the guns would have had no opportunity of killing any tanks.

Written in the form of a cold statement of facts it may sound an inglorious story, but one must give due weight to the circumstances, the actions of other troops around them and the fact that all of them had been in action day in, day out, for thirty days without a break, and the mental and nervous strain of such an experience is considerable.

After we had collected what clothing and food we could find in KL, which was being evacuated at the time, we boarded the Singapore night mail, expecting to arrive there the following morning.

Unfortunately, the driver was a volunteer and didn't know his engine; when dawn came, we had moved about 15 miles. The Japanese air force was paying a good deal of attention to the railway at this time, so the realization that we should now have a 250-mile journey in daylight caused us to keep an eye open for planes. Sure enough, at about 11 o'clock, while we were standing in a wayside station called Tebong some miles north of Gemas, there were shouts from troops in the next coach. We put our heads out of the window to see four twin-engined bombers about 400ft up, turning to fly down the length of the train. Troops and civilians were already jumping out and dashing towards cover under nearby trees. We all jumped pretty quickly then and followed suit. By now the planes were approaching, two on each side of the train, and bombs were falling from them.

I realized I couldn't run fast enough to get off the line if attacked, and as I saw a bomb leave one plane and come directly at me I dived behind a little hut with the thought that I was 'for it' this time. There was a crash and I thought how curious it felt to be dead, then I gave a sort of guffaw of laughter – I realized I wasn't dead and, still more surprising, I wasn't even touched; the bomb had fallen just at the other side of my hut, less than 5yds from me and so close that the bits had gone over my head. One of our subalterns, Bob Hartley, had been with me five seconds before but had thrown himself down on the bank above me; he, poor lad, was killed instantly.

When I picked myself up it was to see an awful shambles. Nine of my officers and men were killed and about a dozen wounded, as well as probably thirty or forty Indians and Asiatic civilians, and many more were injured. We formed a first aid centre and our MO, 'Doc' Tomlinson, worked like a hero. All he had was some morphia for the worst cases and bandages improvised on the spot. He did noble work until doctors and ambulances could be got, which took about two hours.

We buried our men where they fell, there was nothing else to be done, and the wounded were taken off in ambulances.

A breakdown gang arrived, and though the engine had a bullet through its boiler, several coaches were derailed and all the windows were broken, some of the train and the survivors continued their journey, arriving at Singapore the next morning, twenty-four hours late. There we were put in a rest camp by the sea for two days, and we needed it; most of us were a bit strung up after five days of pretty violent and unpleasant happenings.

The last month of active participation in the Malayan Campaign is a depressing little story of withdrawal mile by mile and finally almost yard by yard, until at the end many guns were firing their last reserve of ammunition from the seafront round Raffles Hotel and from the grass plot surrounding the cathedral.

The last days of Singapore hold vivid memories of the frequent roar of concentrations of bombs falling on the defenceless areas of the city as flights of Jap bombers flew over us with no opposition other than a few troops of 3.7 Heavy Ack Ack, while those who came lower were fiercely and sometimes successfully attacked by the lighter calibre Bofors.

Fires in the dock area and blazing oil tanks cast a pall of black smoke by day and a lurid glow by night across the whole southern skyline.

Finally came the unconditional surrender at 4.00 pm on 15 February.

Chapter 3

Into Bondage

Silence after days and weeks of the incessant noise of war seemed almost unnatural, though most of us slept like logs that night for the first time in weeks.

The next two days we spent in collecting scattered members of the Regiment together, and wondering what the Japs had in store for us.

Speculation ran to extremes, but somehow I couldn't imagine them deciding to shoot about 80,000 prisoners, although a few pessimists thought that at least the senior officers might be liquidated. In actual fact, the combatant troops behaved with considerable restraint and we were not molested in any way.

Our first move was to Changi, to which we marched the 12 miles in what seemed a never ending column some 40,000 strong, taking what we could carry and sending very heavy baggage and all the food we could load on to one lorry per unit.

It was a thirsty walk! On arrival we were directed to various areas allocated by Divisions and made the best of limited accommodation in the badly bombed Roberts Barracks, where in peacetime all British troops had been quartered. There was of course no light and hardly any water as most of the mains had been bombed.

We stayed here about a week and the Japs decided that in addition to the area we already occupied, some of us might suitably occupy Changi Gaol about 2 miles down the Singapore road. Our own higher command decided that the 11th Div. Artillery were suitable candidates, so four RA Regiments – including mine – were sent there.

By comparison with later experiences, the gaol was a palace. It consisted of numbers of cells and some large rooms, and we divided the accommodation up between regiments. The whole place was made of concrete, with iron bars, iron gates and iron staircases, but at least it was mostly clean and very soon we cleaned the rest of it. We were allotted the gaol governor's bungalow as well, which I immediately secured for my officers, and that was really very pleasant.

We could go down to the sea about half a mile away and bathe, which was most enjoyable provided one avoided the dead Chinese who kept floating in on every tide; there were three of them one day along about a hundred yards of shore, but we could see them coming so we avoided swimming into them.

The reason for their being there was that the Japs had caught a lot looting – or said they had – and brought several lorry loads up to near where we were and shot them on the shore – *pour encourager les autres*. Our first job on arrival was to bury forty of them, and the Aussies had another sixty or so to deal with – not the most pleasant of jobs.

One Chinese was still alive and was taken up to the British hospital where he recovered and later became an orderly. I don't know how his identity was kept from the Japs, but he was still there several months later, though I don't know the sequel.

We remained in the gaol for a fortnight, and then the Japs decided they wanted us out so that they could put the civilian internees in.

The Japs allotted about four areas to the RA group when we were told to move out of the gaol, and by arrangement with the C.O.s of the other Gunner regiments I took over a group of seaside bungalows on the edge of the Straits of Johore formerly occupied by European business people. These seemed to us the height of luxury as they had a lot of furniture and books still in them, and we all settled in very happily. We found an electric light plant in one of them, got it going and used that one as our officers' quarters and mess. One day some Japs came round and saw it. They were much intrigued and said we could continue to use it if we would run a line to their quarters some distance away. This we undertook to do, but once again, before the job was completed, we were moved, this time to Birdwood Camp in what became 11th Indian Div. area. Before this last move I had found a whole packing case of maps of Malaya in the rubber trees near a former transit camp and collected two which covered all the northern half of the country. On these I marked various places in which 137th Regiment had been in action, and thereby hangs a tale which comes later in the story.

Birdwood Camp was a poor exchange for our bungalows on the seashore, but at least it had huts, and we set about improving on what there was.

We had our Divisional HQ, still commanded by Major General 'Billy' Key – a great man to have around under adverse conditions, always cheerful and full of energy. Under his command, the whole camp some 3,000 strong became highly organized. We made gardens, played cricket, hockey, rugger and soccer on a big cricket ground in the area; arranged lectures, concerts and educational courses and even an infantry tactics Cadre class for officers of each unit to teach jungle warfare, in the event of us being able to become active soldiers again.

Up to the time at which we moved into this area, we had lived largely on the stocks of army rations we had brought with us from Singapore, plus a weekly delivery which the Japs made to us from the godowns in the city which still contained large reserves of European food, mostly in cold storage. To make this spin out, we went to a scale of half rations to keep us going.

Shortly after our arrival in this – apparently – permanent PoW camp, the Japs decided we must learn to eat rice, issued large quantities of it and cut down the meat and flour to next to nothing. We then really knew what it was to be hungry all day. We were unused to rice as a staple diet and most people found they couldn't eat much at first, but we improved with practice.

Our cooks didn't know how to cook rice to the best advantage, which made things no better, and it usually turned out a sodden, soggy mess. We camouflaged it as best we could with faint traces of bully beef, sardines, jam, curry, etc., but they were very faint traces – about one tin of bully beef per forty men. After a few weeks of this we began to suffer from lassitude and diarrhoea. Our latrine accommodation was crude, and the flies and bluebottles alone thrived. This became a serious problem as our MOs knew the danger of a dysentery epidemic. We sprinkled powdered lime around the latrine, made covers of mosquito netting for food and did all we could to safeguard ourselves, but sure enough dysentery appeared and one after another cases were taken to Roberts Hospital – the central hospital for the whole Changi area. Beriberi, the result of lack of vitamins, also appeared, though not in serious numbers.

For recreation, we had the large *padang* or playing field for games; concerts occasionally in the evenings; books, plundered in Singapore and brought back by working parties, with which we formed libraries; debating societies; lectures on diverse subjects by the many experts from every sphere of life in peacetime; and then bridge for those who liked it. At this time I was not a bridge player, but as time went on I decided to learn and thereafter, for the next three years, I played thousands of rubbers and found much enjoyment in it.

The Japs had a wonderful idea about a week after they concentrated us all in the Changi area: they told us to wire ourselves in and supplied us with large quantities of Denert wire. We were given a date by which the job was to be completed, after which they would inspect it. We had to make a double apron fence with a third roll on top of the two bottom ones all round each camp, and gateways on to the main road. They duly inspected this and had thin places thickened up, but in spite of it there was a nightly exodus by numbers of daring characters who went out for the spirit of adventure and to buy food from the local Chinese, which they sold on their return at extortionate prices, thereby creating a flourishing black market.

We were allowed out in organized parties for wood cutting, and I often went on these trips and enjoyed the temporary freedom. I bought eight hens and a cock one day and brought them home in triumph, made them a wire-netting run and then hopefully waited for eggs. They did their stuff all right, and I remember the excitement in the mess the day they laid five eggs; we had an egg each in rotation – a great treat.

For the benefit of those who have not visited the country, perhaps a paragraph or two on weather conditions and climate might help to give a better picture of life as we lived it.

There are virtually no changes of season in Malaya, except that about the end of February – as far as I can remember – the rubber trees and other deciduous trees lose their leaves; but the new growth is so rapid that they are never completely bare, or at any rate there always seemed to be a certain amount of leaf on them.

The temperature is constantly round the 80° mark in the shade and a bit higher in the afternoon. Most of the year round there seemed to be a heavy shower or a thunderstorm, usually in the early afternoon, while during the autumn we had numerous days of heavy rain.

Now and then terrific storms would come over, locally known as 'Sumatras', probably because they came from that direction. Great black clouds would suddenly roll up accompanied by a gale and vivid lightning and thunder. Then the rain would start and pour down in an almost solid sheet of water. In about ten minutes the big 'monsoon' drains would be raging torrents and water would be standing inches deep in any hollow. They usually cleared off in about an hour and then the sun would come out and everything steamed in the heat. By the next morning the ground looked as if it hadn't rained for a week.

The climate is very enervating in consequence of so much damp heat, and in ordinary times Europeans used to find it necessary to take a holiday in the hills where there were hotels and bungalows built to cater for the purpose.

Those with longer experience in Malaya may criticise this brief outline, but such is my impression written after a lapse of years.

In the early days of our woodcutting expeditions we were allowed to bathe in the sea which was grand, and we spent hours either in the lovely warm water or lying on the sand sunbathing; but then the Japs decided we were enjoying ourselves too much and ordered us to stop bathing which was a sad blow, but even then we managed a quick bathe while members of the party kept watch for approaching Japs. There wasn't much risk as the Japs seldom came our way.

Another useful object during our expeditions was the collection of large numbers of coconuts, which we stored and used in our diet with much success.

Our cooks improved rapidly in the culinary art of rice camouflage and learnt how to make bread and cake out of ground rice flour flavoured with coconuts and anything else that would lend itself.

We had a C of E Padre and an RC one in our area, and made plans with the C of E Padre for building a church out of the material from a bungalow on the shore which we proceeded to dismantle.

Prior to this, I devoted part of one of our wooden barrack huts to the holding of services, and every Sunday we had crowded services morning and evening, as well as Holy Communion before breakfast.

Various people contributed to the fabric with things like a counterpane, which someone had acquired as bedding at some time, for an altar cloth. Another man made two very nice wooden candlesticks and others made benches. We brought flowers in from the gardens of deserted houses, and lots of men found peace and comfort in our little chapel at odd times of the day.

From this chapel grew a more ambitious scheme for the building of a small church as already mentioned, but although much material had been collected on the site before I moved up to Siam, I believe it was never completed owing to the movement of large numbers of us to other parts.

During these first few months, sickness was not too bad, but I was unfortunate enough to be among the early victims of bacillary dysentery and was carted off on a stretcher to Roberts Hospital. The hospital was in the ruins of Roberts Barracks, concrete blocks of buildings blasted by pattern bombing during the campaign. Water was very limited and the staff were overworked. One must remember that in addition to cases of sickness, all the battle casualties had been transferred there too; at a guess I should say there must have been 2,000 cases to deal with.

The treatment for dysentery was starvation and Epsom salts three times a day as far as I can remember – for the first five days. It was absolute hell! However, it worked a cure, although I lost about 4 stone in a fortnight and was reduced to a feeble wreck, from which I slowly recovered during the next couple of months. After that experience I took no chances for the next three years over food and discarded anything on which a bluebottle had settled. I am thankful to say I was successful in avoiding any further attacks.

Some time in June we were told that large parties would shortly be leaving for an unknown destination. I was detailed by General Key to make up a working battalion of 500 men from my own regiment and another RA unit. Having done this, after careful medical grading by the MOs, we got orders to move 3,000. We were to move in six trainloads at intervals of two days, each battalion to be commanded by a lieutenant colonel and to have about thirty officers.

As luck would have it, I suddenly developed dengue fever – a virulent fever which runs a high temperature for about five days accompanied by aches and pains all over. The fever then suddenly goes, but by that time one is feeling pretty limp, and under our circumstances it took a week or two to get reasonably fit again.

General Key and Brigadier Rush, our CRA, used to come and visit me every day, and having decided that I couldn't be fit again in time, the general decided to send Major Gill up in charge of my party and gave him local rank as lieutenant colonel to conform to Jap requirements.

So off went my 330 fit men of the 137th Field plus 170 of 80th Anti-tank, and I remained behind to go up as a Supernumerary Lieutenant Colonel with the last party to leave a week later.

On 26 June I left with a battalion from another area commanded by Lieutenant Colonel Williamson of 1st Indian HAA Regiment RA. There were one or two officers in the party whom I knew, and we set off for Singapore in lorries with all our baggage and cooking pots.

We were told we would be twenty-five to a 'carriage' on the train; we were, but the 'carriages' were steel cattle wagons. We sat on the floor like sardines in a tin for five days and four nights while we traversed 1,300 miles of Malaya and Siam. At least, most of us did, but I and three others took a poor view of this after the first two days and nights, and at one of our frequent stops we made ourselves much more comfortable in a baggage truck on top of a pile of valises.

Even so, it was a nightmare journey. The Japs provided us with meals of rice and watery stew, morning and evening. At various stations where we stopped to let other trains pass, since it was otherwise a single-line track, the Tamils and Chinese crowded on to the platforms and gave or sold us eggs, bread, fruit and all sorts of things we hadn't seen for months. From the feeding point of view we did wonderfully well. At one place near the Siamese border the engine stopped for water by a lake, and immediately practically all of us streamed out of the train, threw off our clothes and rushed in for a glorious swim. We had one or two hasty shower baths at other places under the canvas water pipes with which the engine boilers were filled.

At last, on the fifth day, we reached Ban Pong in Siam and detrained. We fell in, in threes, humping as much stuff as we could carry, and marched through the town to the wonderful camp with its completely fitted-out hospital about which our Jap guards had told us.

Chapter 4

A Poor Exchange

W e arrived at the 'wonderful camp with its hospital completely equipped', as promised by the Japanese in Singapore. In England the RSPCA would have brought proceedings against anyone keeping cattle in such a place, but it was good enough for British prisoners of war destined to act as coolies for the next three years in the construction of the Japanese military railway linking Bangkok and Moulmein through 350 miles of virgin jungle by way of the 'Three Pagodas' pass between Siam and Burma.

Outside the entrance to this cattle kraal we were halted and allowed to sit on the side of the road while the Japanese detailed accommodation to the Battalion Commander, Colonel Williamson. About an hour later, we were marched in and detailed to our huts.

These were made of bamboo with *attap* (palm leaf) roofs. They were each about 50yds long, 20ft wide, and 15ft high at the apex, and about 4yds apart. At one end at right angles to them were long lines of latrines about 3yds from the ends of the huts, shallow trenches with *attap*-roofed bamboo shutters over them. The stench was indescribable, and I thanked my stars that my billet was at the farthest end of our hut from them – even though it was bad enough there.

There were twelve huts in a line, with a perimeter fence of bamboo closely surrounding the lot, thus allowing no space for exercise except in front between the huts and the Japanese guardroom at the entrance, where there was a parade ground.

Each hut held 200 people, one for officers and the remainder for the men. Down each side of a centre gangway about 6ft wide ran raised wooden boarded platforms about 2ft high. They were 7ft wide and on them we were allotted a width of about 3ft per man. Here we slept, ate, dressed and kept all our worldly possessions.

There was no water in the camp; we had to walk down the road with a bucket to a well near cookhouses about 200yds distant and were only allowed one bucketful per day.

After the comparative luxury of Changi, these surroundings went as near to 'getting me down' as anything before or since, but I thereupon made up my mind that I would never allow that to happen, and after the realization that if one succumbed to despair one's chance of survival were small, I found myself able to laugh at the conditions. They were so frightful that there were only two alternatives – either to give way to depression or to regard the whole situation as crazy and realize that so long as one survived there would eventually be an end to it.

An extract from my diary written on 5 July 1942 gives a description of the day's routine:

> We get up at 7.30 hours: 8.00 Roll Call out on the road which runs past the entrance to this cattle pen. After that we shave and wash in about 1½ pints of water and clean our teeth in chlorinated water from our water bottles. 09.00 hours breakfast – usually rice and vegetable stew. After that we kill time till 1.30 when rice and vegetable stew appears again. We then kill more time until 6.30 pm (with a Dixie of tea without milk at 4.00 pm) when supper arrives consisting of – what do you think? – rice and vegetable stew! But it generally has a little, very little, meat in it this time. Roll call out on the road again at 9.00 pm, and lights out at 10.00 pm.

My own Regiment, who had preceded me up to Ban Pong, were in a similar camp about 200 yards down the road, but though I made great efforts with the Jap interpreter to let me transfer to them, I was not allowed to do so.

Soon after this, Colonel Williamson was made camp commandant and I took over his battalion of 588 men and 53 officers from about six different regiments. There were a lot of first rate fellows, and I made many friendships which have lasted to this day. There were also some – among the officers – who followed the line of least resistance, groused continually, lost their self-respect and gradually degenerated into useless drones in a community where there was need and opportunity for every man to give of his best in the cause of his fellow men.

Among my earliest friendships at Ban Pong were three doctors – two Scots and one Irishman – and a little Jewish dentist, one of the most likeable and cheerful people I have ever known. Another lasting friend and one for whom I have the greatest admiration of all I met was the Revd R. J. Thompson,

Archdeacon of Singapore Cathedral. An Australian, fifty-nine years old at the time, he was taken prisoner as chaplain to a battalion of the Federated Malay State Volunteers. He maintained an outlook of unconquerable optimism throughout the next three years. 'Padre' Thompson was beloved by all men, and in later days when my responsibilities and problems became heavier, I found him a wise counsellor and one to whom one could open up one's heart on any subject with the certain knowledge of sympathetic hearing and sound advice. There could be few men among the thousands who could not count themselves richer for having known him.

About the middle of July, three men in the 2nd Battalion the Loyal Regiment, and belonging to my battalion, decided to make a break for freedom. They left one night with a supply of food and little else, but their freedom was short-lived. They floundered about in swamps and jungle all night and the next day, then being completely lost gave themselves up to some Siamese and were brought back. They were put to stand in front of the Jap guardroom for the best part of several days as far as I can remember, with long periods when they had to stand to attention. Then they were taken off to Bangkok for a court martial. I endeavoured to persuade the Japs to let a British officer defend them but was told it was impossible. We never heard what happened to them until about two years later, when one of them turned up again on my ship on the way home. They had all been sent to Singapore Gaol with long sentences. Two survived but the other died. Having heard first-hand stories of Singapore and other gaols, it seems wonderful that anyone survived.

The result of the escape bid was a terrific 'flap' on the part of the Japs, who summoned Colonel Williamson to the office and tried to make him sign a paper saying he would not try to escape and would stop anyone else from attempting to. When he refused, they told him he would be shot and that they had sent for the firing party. Then they sent for the three battalion commanders and told us the same thing. We all refused to sign, and finally they gave up the attempt. The firing party didn't appear either.

In July, the generous IJA (Imperial Japanese Army) decided to reward all officers and warrant officers who worked with the handsome remuneration of 25 cents per day, and 10 cents for other ranks. As I was by this time taking daily working parties out on road construction, I received this emolument.

Fortunately, I had had a windfall at Changi. One day after a bathe I was walking along the shore when I saw a notecase floating in close to the shore. I picked it up and found it contained 114 Malay Straits dollars (worth 2/8d each in sterling). As I had entered my PoW existence with only 10 dollars, it was indeed a windfall. I imagine it had belonged to some victim of the war or else to one of the Chinese of whom about sixty had been shot near the spot.

I gave 50 dollars to the regimental funds and kept the rest, and it stood me in good stead before we went up to Siam as I was able to lay in a store of razor blades sufficient to last with careful use and sharpening until we were set free, also shaving soap and other valuable odds and ends such as needles and cotton, two packs of cards, a reserve of tinned bully beef and condensed milk – about two tins of each – and some tobacco.

The climate up here at this time of the year seemed pleasanter than in Malaya. Although rather hotter, it wasn't so enervating and rainy. There were lovely butterflies with vivid colouring, though whatever induced anything so beautiful to fly amid the stench and squalor of our cattle pen, heaven knows!

The first man to succumb to PoW life in our camp died on 20 July and we buried him in the Chinese burial ground nearby. The Japs had a coffin made for him, and their Camp Commandant, Lieutenant Fukui, attended the funeral. We didn't want him there, but I suppose he meant well.

All this time we had been trying to get drugs, dressings and equipment out of them for a hospital, for which one of the end huts was set apart. Here our heroic and hapless doctors dealt with cases of malaria, dysentery, beri-beri in mild form compared to the subsequent cases, accidental injuries and wholesale diarrhoea, which was common to most people from time to time. They had hardly any equipment and few drugs, practically no quinine for malaria, and most of the troops had no mosquito nets. The IJA were dilatory to the point of exasperation and made one excuse after another, but meanwhile the sick rate steadily increased.

The local Siamese, or Thais as they called themselves in those days, were more friendly; they were also out to trade for their own benefit and gave the Japs a lot of trouble carrying out black-market deals with us through the perimeter fence. Occasionally one was caught, brought to the guardroom and unmercifully beaten and kicked by all the guards and any other Jap who cared to join in. They were then usually tied up to a post and kept there in the sun, sometimes for one day and sometimes for several, while any Jap or

Korean guard as likely as not would give them a kick or a blow with his rifle as he passed. It was a revolting business for us to witness and in the early days we booed and hissed at the Japs, but we soon found that only made them more vicious and that the best thing to do was to keep out of sight so that they had no gallery to play up to. I have even seen Thai women tied up in the same way, though they were not treated as roughly as the men, but badly enough.

The road construction upon which the men were employed was our first experience of the primitive method of construction with a large labour force employed by the Japanese in this kind of work. Every morning, two or three of the battalions would parade and having been issued with spades, shovels, *chunkols* (a kind of large-size hoe) and baskets rather like gardeners use for brushing up leaves, at the rate of about one tool to each two men, we would march along the road for about a mile to a point where a muddy or dusty track – according to weather – led across some *padi* fields to a small *kampong* (village or a collection of a few native huts). Here, after much shouting and gesticulating and some very difficult conversation with the so-called inter-preter, the officer in charge (myself or one of the other COs) would get a rough idea of what was required, which we would then pass on to the officers in charge of companies. The procedure was to dig earth from the ground at either side of the proposed road, filling the baskets which were then carried by two men and emptied on the track, gradually building up a raised embankment which was roughly levelled by other men. The constant stream of men coming and going with their baskets substituted for a steam roller.

We got breaks of about ten minutes every hour when the Jap interpreter would yell in his fluent English, '*Oru men resto*' – 'oru' being as near as a Jap could get to 'all'. During these 'restos' the local Thais did a roaring trade in bananas and eggs, often to the annoyance of the Japs, who disapproved of this fraternization.

These eggs and the hundreds and thousands, or more probably millions, we bought in the next three years were the saving of many men's lives. They were ducks' eggs of which there are thousands in Siam. They do keep hens, but in very small numbers, and their eggs are only about the size of a ban-tam's. Once one got used to the rather fishy flavour of the ducks' eggs, one thrived on them. I always feel a great affection for ducks now and am very doubtful if I should be writing this if it hadn't been for the gallant Siamese ducks!

I am one of the very few people who in 3½ years never had his face slapped by some irate Korean guard or Japanese soldier; but on one occasion during the road-making period I came very near to receiving this insulting treatment.

Towards the end of a rather long day's work, when the men had had enough, I conveyed to the Jap interpreter the fact that I thought it was time we went home. He had a conversation with the NCO in charge of operation and then told me we could go when a certain place was level. The Jap NCO could speak a few words of English so I said to him, 'Ten more baskets – all men go home?' and he replied with the usual 'OK'. Consequently, after counting the baskets of earth dumped, I told the men to collect their tools and fall in. The interpreter flew into a rage and came up yelling '*koorah*' – the Japanese word for 'come here, you' and their usual method of address when annoyed. I hadn't a clue what it was all about and stood and stared at him. He then accused me in English of having stopped the men working without an order, and I explained about the 'ten more baskets' and that the other Jap had agreed. He told me I was lying, and each time I told him I wasn't. All the time he was getting angrier and angrier. I continued to look him in the eye and then just when I was quite certain I was going to get one across the cheek, he regained control of himself and said we could go home.

I had similar experiences with them on many subsequent occasions and always found that by keeping one's eyes fixed on theirs, one could finally stare them out. It may have been also that I was about two feet taller than most of them that helped, but the fact remained that in all my dealings I was never hit by one.

As time went on, cases of men having their faces slapped became more frequent, and each time we protested to the Camp Commandant, but it didn't usually make much difference. In the IJA it is the normal reaction of one soldier to another whenever the junior commits any act of which the senior disapproves. The matter is dealt with on the spot without any kind of enquiry. Any senior or any other rank can hit his junior, and the one in the wrong has to 'take it'. There is no retaliation, or if there is, the consequences are much worse and the offender gets set upon and beaten up by all the other Japs round about.

It can be appreciated, therefore, that what seemed degrading and insulting treatment to us was the natural order of things to them, and there were so many incidents of this kind that that after a time we came to accept it as the natural consequence of any act of which they might disapprove. Nevertheless, we always protested on principle and sometimes were successful in getting it at least reduced to a minimum for a time. It entirely depended upon the attitude of the then Camp Commander.

One day there was a rather more serious incident when a party were sent to do hut building at a nearby Japanese military camp. Some trouble arose and a Japanese sergeant hit a British officer across the face with a bamboo stick. On his return, the British officer in charge reported it, and Colonel Williamson went to complain; evidently some notice was taken, because on the following day I took a party to continue the work and when we arrived a different Jap sergeant was in charge. I detailed the men to the job and the Jap sergeant came over to me and said, 'Me no hit British soldiers, me Japanese gentleman.' He kept his word, anyhow!

After a month or two at Ban Pong we got to know that a railway was to be constructed, starting from Ban Pong and going north to the Burma border. The Japanese Colonel, Yanagita by name, who was about 4ft 6ins high and wore the 1918 Victory Medal ribbon among his Japanese ones, made us a terrific speech standing on a table in the middle of our parade ground. It was all in Japanese, of which we could not understand a word, and it was then translated into very different English by the interpreter. It was mostly promises of better conditions and an exhortation to obey the Japanese rules: not to try to escape and 'to keep ourselves well and eat much'. We were further exhorted to 'bring this speech to the very bottoms of your soldiers'.

For months we had repeatedly asked to be allowed to write letters home; it was the one thing everyone wanted more than anything else. While we were in Changi, General Percival had succeeded at last in getting permission for us to send postcards, which we wrote early in June. Some 1,100 I believe, out of about 50,000 got home in October, and mine was one of them. In these we were allowed to say how we were in our own words, but to disclose no details of our location. Here, however, the Japanese refused to give us permission to write home and it wasn't for months that we were allowed to send the next postcards.

We were not devoid of all contact with the outside world. Some bold and enterprising officers had brought a wireless set up from Changi in a dismantled state, put it together again in Ban Pong and got it working. They kept it under the bed space of one of them, where it was very easy for an inquisitive Jap to find; but at this time we had no great reason to fear very evil consequences even if it was found, although it was expected that it would result in confiscation and some face slapping. All went well until one day the Japs startled us by ordering everyone out of their huts. This was obviously the prelude to a search, but their technique was not as highly developed as it became later on, and the officer under whose bed the set reposed pretended to have an urgent call of nature, ran back into the hut, wrapped the set up in some clothing and bolted to the latrines, where he dumped it until the search was over.

As far as I can remember, the searchers took very little, but always a few odds and ends were missed by their owners, though, curiously, in spite of many evil traits of character, the Korean guards and Jap NCOs respected ownership of private possessions so long as they had no potential value as weapons.

The Japanese Colonel became quite hospitable on one or two occasions and invited the COs to eat fruit and drink tea in his house while we held a joint conference through the Interpreter Adachi (a horrible little reptile who had been employed in a British insurance company's office in Tokyo). At one of these conferences he told us the purpose of the proposed railway was 'to develop the rich properties of the hinterland'.

About the end of September we had a most unpleasant experience: it poured a deluge of tropical rain for hours on end one night and we woke up to find the entire camp under water of varying depths up to about 2ft. Boots and bits of equipment were floating about in every direction, though fortunately my own had sunk and I retrieved them by feeling about in a foot of filthy water under my bed.

It is difficult to convey a description on paper: 1,800 men living in 2 acres, all having to splash through dirty mud and water every time they got out of their beds. The latrines had likewise filled with water and their contents had mingled with it. The whole place stank of excrement, but through all this we splashed barefooted out on various errands and duties.

The water softened the ground and huts began to lean at crazy angles; several collapsed altogether, necessitating speedy evacuation into other already crowded huts by the unfortunate occupants, who usually lost a good many possessions in the disaster.

We took out working parties and dug ditches to try and drain the flood, but there was so little fall that this was only partially successful. However, after about two days the water receded from most of the area, leaving an expanse of soft, slippery mud with the most awful stink imaginable.

During this disaster I visited the so-called hospital several times. Words cannot describe the conditions there. Heroic doctors and orderlies splashed barefooted from patient to patient lying 6ins above the reeking water. Men suffering from malaria, dysentery, skin disease, fractured limbs and tropical ulcers lay uncomplaining amid these frightful conditions. Medical supplies and drugs were entirely inadequate. At one end of the hut a space was reserved as dispensary, surgery and operating theatre. Night and day, the tired doctors and orderlies carried on undefeated in their mission in conditions beyond description. Men began to die, one or two each week. Small wonder, in such surroundings and with a lack of vital medicine. They were buried in the Chinese cemetery down the road with all reverence and such honour and tribute as we could pay them under our restricted conditions.

And so life continued during the remainder of September and into October, until the day came for those of us who were fit enough to make the journey to a new camp nearer the hills beyond a small town called Kanchanburi (pronounced 'Khan-bu-ree'), a distance of some 50km northwest of Ban Pong.

Chapter 5

The Great Trek

Zero hour was 08.00 hours on Friday, 11 October 1942, when a motley crew of some 800 all ranks assembled in battalions on the still muddy parade ground with everything they could hope to carry slung around them, and valises, cooking pots and other heavy gear dumped in piles awaiting transport by lorry.

We had urged the Japs for days about the number of men who had no boots left and therefore could not march, and about those who were sick and unfit to make the journey; but it cut no ice, and ultimately only those who were in hospital were left behind and everyone else was ordered to march – boots or no boots! They ordered us to take the boots of the men in hospital and give them to others, which seemed a bit unfair, but there appeared to be nothing for it but to do so.

Our first day's march was to be 21km, but like most Japanese promises it proved to be something longer and was in fact 29 km, or about 18 miles. In a temperature of 90°, ill-shod, ill-fed, overloaded and reduced in stamina by six months of this existence, it was no mean feat that about 90 per cent of us completed the course. On arrival at the staging camp we found the Jap administration had failed as usual and the party of cooks who had been sent ahead in a lorry had been used for cutting wood and in camp chores for the Jap occupants of the camp; we had to sit on the side of the road for three hours waiting for the usual meal of rice and vegetable stew.

In spite of everything, we were all remarkably cheerful. The very fact of leaving that awful stinking cattle pen and getting away into clean air and new surroundings, as well as a certain quite exciting anticipation of the unknown future, had a brightening effect upon everyone.

The next morning we started off again bright and early at 9.00 am and only had to march a mere 12km to the next staging camp, though this was far enough for those with blistered feet. This camp was much too small and we were crowded 'like sardines', as the Jap interpreter accurately described it; once again, we sat about for hours waiting for our food, owing to the lorry with the cooks on board having been taken to the wrong camp.

Next morning, reveille was at 6.30 am, and those of us who were lucky enough to be in huts woke up to find it pouring with rain. Those who slept outside probably woke earlier! After a wet breakfast and packing up of wet blankets, we started the third and final stage of our journey. We marched 12 kms to Kanburi, where we had a good long rest in the middle of the day. We did rather well here for food as the Japs issued quite a lot of tins of M & V [meat and vegetables] with our rice, and there were scores of Siamese selling fruit, bananas, and nauseating little concoctions cooked in *qualis* on charcoal fires which we consumed with avidity nevertheless – anything for a change from plain rice and stew! I should explain that a *quali* is the local container for all sorts of cooking. It is a cast iron boiler cum frying pan shaped like a saucer. There are all sizes, big ones such as we used in our camp cookhouse, about 3ft in diameter and 18ins deep, and little ones used by the Thais in their houses or wayside stalls about 18ins in diameter and 4ins deep. Ovens and saucepans as we know them were unknown in Siamese culinary circles.

Kanburi is one of the oldest towns in Siam. The original town was contained inside a fortified wall made of limestone and mortar about 15ft high. The wall enclosed an area of 3 or 4 acres and was in a remarkably good state of preservation, although reputed to be seventeenth century. The town today has spread all around and has a population of somewhere in the neighbourhood of 7,000 to 8,000, I should imagine.

Situated on the banks of the Quainoy [Kwai Noi] river at the point where the Quaiyai [Kwai Yai] joins it, the scene is very picturesque. The broad river is a mass of flat-bottomed barges, puffing little motorboats and native canoes. Scores of children spend their day in and out of the water, clad only in their brown skins, the little girls wearing a small affair of woven silver rather like a tiny sporran slung round their waists to satisfy convention. The normal dress for those over eight years old is a pair of shorts for the boys and a sarong and blouse for the girls.

All the commercial traffic of the district is carried by barge. Some are punted by two men with long bamboo poles, others are towed up and down the two rivers in strings of anything up to half a dozen by sturdy little motor boats with diesel engines, referred to always as 'pom-poms'.

In due course we were all loaded into barges, about 30 men to each, and towed up the Quainoy for a couple of miles. After the dreary flat country around Ban Pong and the expanse of mud in which we had existed for months, this lovely broad river with blazing sunshine, vivid green forest and red clay banks brought us nearer to a feeling of freedom than any of us had experienced since we became prisoners.

Enormous and vividly coloured butterflies fluttered over the water and among the bushes on either bank; birds which were strange to most of us skimmed the water or flew along the banks; and here and there were little palm-roofed shacks perched on the banks, each one the home of a family of Thais, with children playing in canoes and in the water and often the women of the household doing the family washing in the river.

After about half an hour we pulled in to the left bank, where there was a rough wooden jetty and steps cut out of the red earth leading up the bank through dense clumps of bamboo. A number of Korean soldiers, members of the Japanese camp staff, stood waiting to watch us disembark, springing to attention with a strange cry which we afterwards learnt to know as '*Kiot-ake!*' or the Japanese for 'Attention!' as the Jap Colonel Yanagida stepped ashore.

We had arrived at Chungkai Camp.

We unloaded our baggage on to the bank and marched along a shady path for several hundred yards to the camp, which we were told was ready and waiting for us. We reached a large clearing and saw three long huts complete, piles of bamboo poles on the ground and heaps of *attap* palm for roofing; this was the 'finished' camp for 800 plus the 60 who had been sent on three weeks before to build it.

The three huts would hold 600, so many people slept in the open for the next few nights. Fortunately, the weather was fine so it was no great hardship, and we were used to roughing it by now. There were no cookhouses and no latrines. The latter were our first task, and the cooks continued to work in the open on the river bank.

The fact that the camp was not ready for us was not the fault of the advance party. As soon as they arrived they had been diverted from their intended task to that of quarrying the beginning of a cutting through a rocky spur through which the railway was to run. The Jap engineers had priority when it came to a question of work-parties, so they just commandeered our fellows from the PoW organization, and such of the camp as was ready when we arrived had been built by cooks and a few less fit men left in camp.

We all set to work to build huts for the next few weeks. Great rafts of bamboo poles lashed together were floated down the river by Thais, who cut them higher up and steered the barges downstream with long poles. Many of these rafts had little huts built on them, in which the 'crew' lived during their journey downriver. Pom-poms towed barges upriver to the camp packed high with sheets of *attap* palm roofing material. This came from the lower regions of the country as there were no *attap* palms where we were. The sheets were ingeniously contrived: first a piece of split cane about 3ft long and an inch wide, over which was bent a long *attap* palm leaf, the leaf being roughly stitched with some sort of rattan.

In constructing the roof of a hut, the 'rafters' of bamboo were set about 18ins apart and, starting at the eaves, a sheet was laid across them and tied with rattan. The next sheet was laid about 4ins higher up, and so on. The result was a completely waterproof thatch when well made. Unfortunately, they weren't always well made, as we often found to our cost in the rainy season.

Such was our arrival at this earthly paradise, as it was described to us before leaving Ban Pong. Certainly it did measure up to that description when compared with the Augean stables in which we had existed for the last three months.

Chapter 6

Pastures New

My own arrival at Chungkai was marked by a major tragedy. Our 'heavy baggage', i.e. valises etc., had been sent up by lorry to Kanburi and thence in barges towed by pom-poms up to Chungkai. The evening we arrived, I was too busy at first getting my battalion sorted out and bedded down to think about my own valise, and when I did find time it was almost dark. I went to the river bank, where there were piles of kit lying around, but couldn't find it anywhere. Next morning, I returned to the search and by the river bank found one valise – mine, opened and ransacked. Nearly everything had been stolen: boots, socks, stockings, slacks, a sheet, towels, soap, tinned food and various odds and ends. In fact I was left with my camp bed and a blanket, a change of shirt, shorts and socks, as these had been in my pack, and the bed I had carried with me to the camp. Otherwise all I had was my empty valise and one or two odds and ends the thieves hadn't bothered to remove.

Fortunately, I had a few dollars left out of my treasure trove picked up in the sea at Changi and with this I bought as many essentials as I could from other people who had more kit and less cash, but it was a bitter blow at this stage. I had also hung on to my leather attaché case throughout the journey which contained my most treasured belongings: a book of snapshots of home, a bible, razor blades, two packs of cards, my diary to date, a bottle of aspirins and a few little odds and ends.

About this time we heard that two hospital ships had arrived at Singapore with Red Cross supplies for us. This was in fact true, but it was all distributed to people down there – after the Japs had had their whack nothing ever arrived for us.

As the new camp was merely a clearing in the jungle there were no fences to keep us in, though the Japs said we were not to speak to Thais. However, this did not stop us buying fruit and eggs from the numerous itinerant vendors who appeared in dozens in the next few days, set up little shelters round the camp and did a roaring trade. After a day or two the Japs saw it was no use trying to stop us fraternizing with the Thais and gave up bothering. We even found they didn't seem to mind us going for walks in the jungle; many of us promptly took advantage, and very pleasant it was too.

One night, a doctor and I went and watched the first native 'sing-song' we had seen. One Thai sat cross-legged on the ground playing a kind of xylophone made of wood with very little tone: a range of about an octave and a half. Another beat a tom-tom incessantly, and several more sat hitting two sticks together. To the accompaniment of this jazz band, a party of children danced, singing incomprehensible words; at frequent intervals, when they appeared to forget their words, they just sang 'Ni-Ni-Ni' on two notes interminably.

Soon after we got here, another party arrived from Singapore and told us about their unpleasant experience when several thousands were herded into Salarang Barracks for five days and nights, at a density of approximately a million men to the square mile, because they refused to sign a similar undertaking to the one they had tried to make us sign at Ban Pong. During these five days, men lived, cooked, ate, slept, performed their natural functions, and also died, in this Black Hole of Calcutta. At the end of it, their determination not to sign was as strong as ever, but the Japs then ordered the 2,000 sick and wounded to be brought from Roberts Hospital to join them, and that altered the situation. In the face of this threat, the order was given by the senior British colonel to sign. After all, what did it matter? If one signed and then tried to escape one would be shot if captured; and if one didn't sign, the result would be the same.

I remember so well making an entry in my diary at about this time on the subject of '*lebensraum*' [living space]. My diary was written in the form of a letter to my wife. It read as follows:

> You always said I could never be happy if I had to leave Newland and live in a cottage. Well, at the moment I am living in an area 7ft by 2ft 6ins and that contains my camp bed, and everything has to live on it or under it. I shall appreciate the spaciousness of Newland when I see it.

I did.

At the end of the October the IJA announced the new rates of pay which they proposed to give to officers. As a lieutenant colonel I drew (nominally) $220 a month, from which they deducted $45 for food and maintenance, then paid us all $30 in cash and credited the balance to accounts opened in our names in the Yokohama Specie Bank, which they were careful to inform us was a generous act and one we should appreciate after the war, when we would be able to draw upon it in Japan.

About the end of October 1942, large numbers began to arrive from Singapore to work on the railway. Up to now we had done no more than provide working parties to construct roads and camps for the Jap engineers and cut the railway 'trace' through scrub, but now it was evident that the real job of building the railway was about to start.

Even at this stage, the number of sick was getting disturbingly large. Scabies, beriberi in its early stage, tummy troubles, tropical ulcers on the legs from bamboo scratches and of course the ever present malaria were the main causes of illness, and to cope with this the doctors had part of a hut and hardly any drugs.

We made strong and repeated representations to the Japs for medicine, bandages and better hospital accommodation, with no avail; though at last, when we said that the officers would build a hospital if they provided the materials, they were so surprised that they agreed to do so, and we built two good huts in a clearing a little way away from the main camp which was a great improvement on any previous accommodation for the purpose. But the Japs continued to dole out medical supplies in penny numbers quite inadequate for our requirements, and then only the most elementary things like quinine, potassium permanganate, lysol and about five small bandages per week.

On 11 November I witnessed a strange and unexpected sight. The Jap Colonel had called a conference of British COs for 10.30 am. At 11 o' clock our buglers sounded the Last Post and up jumped the Jap Colonel and his minions and stood at attention for the two minutes' silence as we did! He and I both wore the Victory Medal for the 1914–1918 war too!

By now, our camp numbered about 6,000, and many old friends had arrived up with a fund of cheering stories from Singapore, most of which proved to be purely fictitious; however, they served a useful purpose by perking us all up and renewing hope of an early end to the war.

For several weeks we had been clearing more ground and building a lot more huts, but we never had enough built before more people would arrive; consequently, the last comers nearly always had to sleep out for some time until accommodation could be provided. In the middle of this influx it rained for 36 hours on end and the river rose 15 feet and flooded about half the camp, just to make conditions a bit more uncomfortable; about 2,000 were rendered 'homeless' for several days. In succeeding years we learnt to expect floods at certain times and managed to make some sort of provision which minimized the discomfort, but the first flood was a surprise packet as it happened in the middle of the dry season.

One day, about this time, I experienced an amusing incident over some maps which might have had unpleasant repercussions if the Jap officer concerned hadn't held me in good favour.

I had three maps of Malaya among my possessions, as mentioned earlier in this story, with many of the places marked where my Regiment had been in action. I was hoping to bring them home ultimately. One day I lent them to another officer to look at and he got caught by one of the Korean guards, who wanted to know whose they were. I was out at that time and when I came back I heard about it and was told that the Korean was coming back. When he came (accompanied by two others) he demanded the maps and took them and me in triumph to a Jap officer in search of Osata, the Japanese Adjutant. Osata gave a cursory glance at them and said, 'See me 4 o' clock'. Accordingly, I reported to his office at 4.00 pm, whereupon he unfolded the maps, looked at them for a time and then told the interpreter to ask me when, where and how I had got them, as we weren't allowed to have maps. I told him the answers and showed him some of the places marked where my Regiment had fought in Malaya. He became much interested, particularly when I explained it was an artillery regiment, and said in his very little English, 'Me Artillery'. He then asked (through Adachi, the Interpreter) all about the formation of a gunner regiment, and I drew a diagram showing the CO at the top, majors, captains and subalterns with their batteries and troops. After studying this for a bit, he looked up with a grin and pointing to CO at the top said, 'Your' and then to the subaltern at the bottom and said, 'Me'. After that he gave me a packet of cigarettes and said I could have my maps back 'when a happier day comes'. He was never one of the bad type of Japs, and was one of those who got off without being hanged after the war.

During November, four men went off in the vain hope of escaping. They never had a chance, of course, and early in December, they were caught, but not before they had killed at least one Jap. The day they were found to be missing, all COs were lectured by Colonel Yanagida on the folly and crime of attempting to escape, and we were told to tell our men they would be shot if any of them tried.

The day after we heard they had been captured, the Japs sprang a surprise search on our camp. This occupied most of the morning. The Japs were looking for weapons and maps particularly. They found no arms, but removed a curious assortment of articles which they considered of warlike nature, among which were a map of Salisbury Plain and another of the Battle of Blenheim, which one of them tore out of a book. Fortunately, they didn't take my diary. It was worded fairly innocently, but it would have been disappointing to lose it.

A day or two later our British Quartermaster (a major) asked me to go with him to look at a cow with the Jap QM, who proposed to let us buy one for food. We went miles through the jungle and really had rather a pleasant excursion, except for another little incident which I will recount.

It was a strange party: myself, our QM, the Japs' RSM, the so-called Jap doctor (a warrant officer) and a Siamese. After a long walk we all sat down and smoked the Jap RSM's cigarettes. During this rest, I pulled my handkerchief out of my breast pocket and with it came a folded paper containing a complete secret code which had been sent up to me by hand from a colonel in Singapore, containing also the key to the code, which was to be used in the possible event of a mass escape. Altogether a most incriminating document. The Jap RSM saw it and said, 'What is it?'

Quicker than I could have thought possible I replied, 'Letters from wife – like these,' and produced my pocket book, which contained two or three of the last I had received before we were taken prisoner. I followed this up by producing photos of my family, and he forgot all about the offending document, but the next hour or two were very uncomfortable ones as I thought he might remember and ask to see it, but we got home without further reference to it.

Early in December, a diphtheria epidemic broke out and a number of officers and other ranks died, which added to the despondency of our spirits. It continued for many weeks, of which more anon. During the last month or two work had been going on feverishly on the construction of the railway under the supervision of two of the most hated Jap engineer officers, Taramoto and Kirriama. Taramoto was cold, brutal and remorseless; Kirriama was a plain thug. Both of them knocked men and officers about on numerous occasions and they loathed the British officers because, on principle and under the terms of the Hague Convention, they refused to do manual labour for the Japs, although they did lots for the camp.

Matters came to a head on 20 December. That day, all officers not on administrative work in the camp were ordered to parade at 9.00 am the next day for bridge building. The COs got together and we asked for a conference with the Japs; we explained our reasons and cited the Hague Convention, but they refused to listen and ordered all officers to parade. There was more argument, but Taramoto was out to humiliate the officers and meant to do it. They then ordered all the guards to surround us and told them to train bren guns on us. This began to look serious, and we asked for time for further discussion among ourselves. Another TA colonel and I were for calling their bluff a bit further, but the rest of the COs thought it was unwise, so we agreed to capitulate. Probably they were right. I have often wondered whether the Japs would have dared to fire if we had stood out against it. Anyway, the result was that the whole party were marched off there and then and issued with tools. The COs of course were not included.

Relations were rather more strained than usual after this, and the Japs tightened up a good deal on us. We used to sing 'The King' whenever we had a sing-song, but that was forbidden. They also refused to let us buy from the Thais (it was always forbidden, but frequently winked at) and played hell with any Thais they caught doing anything to which they could object. The usual procedure was to tie the offender up to a post by the guard house and knock him about for hours on end with fists, feet or rifles. If the Thai fainted, they kicked him on the ground, and if that didn't bring him round, they would threw water over him and, when he recovered, make him stand at attention; as soon as they thought he had recovered sufficiently, they would start hitting him again.

How we despised the little yellow devils, but there was nothing we could do about it.

This brought us to our first Xmas in captivity. We had recently formed a choir in connection with the little Bamboo Church we had built, and on Xmas Eve we serenaded the camp with carols. Although the night was a tropical one and our surroundings hardly reminiscent of Xmas at home, our singing was much appreciated and we enjoyed it ourselves.

On Xmas Day we had an extra special meal with a more liberal ration of meat, including some pork which the Japs provided, and a lot of fruit. They also gave us postcards to send home – the first since those we had sent the previous May. They were printed Field Post Cards intended to imitate the British variety. The wording was a comic effort as follows:

I am interned in Thailand.
My health is excellent.
I am ill in hospital.
I am working for pay.
I am not working.
Please see that .... is taken care.
My love to you.
(Signature)

My wife received mine a year later. Our next postcards were written on 15 January 1944.

At least the Japs did give us a holiday for Xmas Day, and we began it with Holy Communion and a morning service. I had been out of the camp the day before and brought back a lot of frangipani branches covered with white flowers, from some trees near a Buddhist temple, with which I decorated the altar and altar rails. Frangipani has a lovely scent, though almost overpowering. The flowers are very like camellias, and it looked very pretty and quite Christmassy. We then had our midday meal and a dog race meeting in the afternoon with wooden dogs and wooden dice. We ran a tote on which I remember winning the large sum of 60 cents on a 10 cent ticket. At 6.00 pm we had our real Xmas Dinner, followed by a rather extra special effort in concerts.

Most of the battalion commanders sent each other handmade Xmas cards drawn and painted or done in crayon by men in their battalions, and I kept several of these of various years and managed to bring them home. Altogether we managed to stage a very fair imitation of Xmas.

The Japs, not being Christians, do not celebrate Xmas, but curiously they make a great celebration of New Year, so we got another holiday that day, though there were no extra rations for us and most people spent it resting and washing themselves and their scanty wardrobe in the river.

About 20 January we were told that several more battalions would move up country very shortly and I was to take mine. Of the original 600 there were comparatively few, owing to drafts having been sent to make up earlier parties and a large number being in hospital. Up to this time there had been 40 deaths in the camp, which at that time we looked upon as a high figure, although compared with the following 12 months it was negligible. Most of these were from malaria, dysentery, general debility and, latterly, diphtheria.

A day or two later there was an unpleasant affair. Eric Lacey, who was Assistant British Camp QM, was being bothered by a stupid little Korean guard who came into his hut and began looking at all Eric's possessions. Quite good naturedly Eric pushed him towards the door, whereupon the Korean got angry, turned round and let fly with his fist. Eric countered it with the flat of his hand against the man's jaw and cut his lip on his front teeth. Out went the guard and returned with a member of the *Kempeitai* [the Japanese equivalent of the Gestapo], who were a complete law unto themselves. This thug dragged Eric out of the hut and set upon him with a heavy stick, beating him all over the body unmercifully. The result was a broken arm and terrible bruises and contusions all over his body from which he fainted. The *Kempeitai* man then seized a passing British OR and told him to hit Eric, which he naturally refused to do and got several belts from the Jap for his refusal.

While this was going on, various people rushed to the Camp Office to tell Colonel Williamson (Camp Commandant) and other officers. When I arrived on the scene Colonel Williamson was being threatened too, so I went off at the double straight to Colonel Yanagida without any ceremony and told him to come and stop it. He grinned at me, as the little so-and-so always did, but did at least send Adachi, the Interpreter, who was effective. Thereupon another friend of Eric's and I carried him to the hospital, where he remained for a month. This was only one case of many, but it shows the type of brutal, sadistic bully with whom we had to deal all the time.

One morning a few days later I awoke with a very sore throat. I walked over to where my friend Ian McIntosh, a Malayan doctor, lived and asked him to look at it. 'I don't like the look of it, you'd better come over to the hospital,' said Mac.

There appeared to be little doubt in the mind of any of the doctors, and I was detailed to take my camp bed, which I had managed to keep with me so far, to the 'Dip' ward; if there was any doubt, it was likely to be dispelled in due course. There I joined a ward of about a dozen officers and thirty men, all in various stages of the disease. The next day I was visited by Dr Hugh de Wardener, who approached me with a villainous looking hypodermic syringe and a nasty looking bottle. This was a cultivation from a pint of blood extracted from one of the other patients who was considered to be sufficiently far removed from death to stand it. He pumped 150cc into my thigh and left it to work its will.

The next few days are rather hazy in my memory, but when I began to appreciate my surroundings again I was aware of a very painful leg, as if I had been kicked by a horse, and of feeling very weak; but the injection had done its work and I was on the road to recovery. About four people died during the next week around me, including the man in the next bed. Immediately he was removed he was replaced by another, who lasted three days and died quite suddenly, just after I had been talking to him. I began to think I was in a bad place.

We were forbidden to get out of bed at all for a month, and during that time eighty of us had to do with one bedpan which, as you may imagine, was in constant demand day and night.

We had magnificent orderlies – Corporal Field RAMC as head orderly and four others by day and two by night, who washed us, brought our meals and drinks, took our temperatures and altogether gave us the most devoted service under awful conditions. Hugh de Wardener was indefatigable too, and we all owe our lives to their unremitting care.

Those of us who became convalescent were able one by one to do a few things to help the others, and it instilled a great spirit of friendship between all ranks. One officer, Lieutenant Kendall, was completely paralysed, could not speak and could only just swallow. For days we thought he was 'a goner', but Corporal Field looked after him like a baby and brought him round, feeding him with a spoon every hour or two.

I had just been allowed up from my bed when I developed jaundice, which set me back a bit and put me off my food. In fact, the only thing I could eat for a few days without feeling sick was plain rice. However, jaundice in a hot climate isn't as bad as in England, thank goodness, and I soon got over that and began to reach the convalescent stage.

The serum which the MOs cultivated from the blood of people with diphtheria proved very successful, and the death rate fell at once from the earlier alarming figures. As soon as I had got over the actual fever stage, I was carried off on a stretcher to what was termed by courtesy the operating theatre, where the MO took a pint from me for the benefit of some other unfortunate, and so on.

The methods of extracting blood and giving a blood transfusion were of necessity somewhat crude. The donor was placed on a bamboo bed with his arm hanging over the side. The needle was then pushed in and a rubber tube attached to it which led into a jam jar standing on the ground. When the jam jar was considered full enough, the needle was taken out and the victim was rewarded with a cup of indifferent tea with sugar as a special treat but, of course, no milk. For a blood transfusion the process was reversed, the jam pot being put on a bamboo stand several feet above the patient so as to create the necessary pressure. All very simple, but it worked.

I was much touched one day when Sergeant Page, one of the sergeants from my battalion cookhouse, appeared with a mess tin of special soup for me which he had concocted from some pork he had obtained somehow, and handed it in to be given to me. Another day he brought along some other delicacy he had contrived. When one realizes how well any of these men could have done with some extra nourishment, it makes the act generous to a degree.

A year later he died in a railway building camp further up country from dysentery and avitaminosis, poor lad.

After about six weeks I was allowed out of hospital, still very weak, but able to walk a short distance slowly. I returned to find most of the 'fit' men of my battalion had been sent up country and the 300 or so who were left were either in hospital or convalescent like me. Gradually I regained strength, spending my time reading and sitting under shady trees.

As I got stronger I felt the necessity for some mild form of occupation with which to pass the time. I joined a friend, Major Jack Riley, who had been an earlier victim of diphtheria, in a small voluntary job of taking bottles of quinine round the malaria wards three times a day and doling out the prescribed number of pills to each patient. At this period the Japanese were providing quite large quantities of quinine pills, which they were then able to obtain from Java. It was the only kind of medical necessity which they ever did supply in any quantity.

By means of this little job we got to know hundreds of men with whom otherwise we should never have had any contact, and the men seemed to look forward to our rounds, during which a lot of harmless banter passed. We used to tell them any little bits of camp gossip or rumours which we felt might brighten them up, and it was wonderful how much a few words and a joke seemed to cheer them.

Diphtheria had a curious effect afterwards on many people in that it paralysed various muscles. In addition to Kendall, who was completely paralysed even to the extent of hardly being able to swallow and being rendered completely speechless for weeks, others were affected in their toes, legs and fingers. The only thing I found was that the end joints of both my little fingers were paralysed and insensible to pain for about a month, but everyone threw it off ultimately as far as I can remember.

While I was still in hospital, a small colony of Siamese who lived in a *kampong* just outside the camp celebrated the hundredth day after the death of one of their number. On this day the spirit of the dear departed is supposed to make its journey to paradise, and in order to guard it from all evil spirits on its way the relatives hold a feast and a non-stop dance-cum-sing-song, which goes on interminably, with dancing, the beating of tom-toms, blowing of horns and weird wind instruments and singing of ceaseless incantations which rise and fall in semi-tones in a highly limited range. This one went on without stopping for 17 hours, and you can imagine how we who were in all stages of illness enjoyed it.

Either the birds in this country take their cue from the inhabitants, or vice versa, and so do the big lizards called 'geckos'. At any rate, they also make monotonous sounds on about two notes like English cuckoos, but less tunefully. The gecko seems to wind himself up with a noise very similar to a clock and then goes off into a series of 'Geck-o's', each one getting a little fainter and slower, until at the fifth or sixth he usually utters a faint 'Geck' and evidently hasn't enough breath left for the 'o'. It is amusing at first, but after an hour or so it becomes quite maddening.

There was a smaller lizard – a kind of chameleon – which had a long thin tail which used to fall off if you picked it up by it. Presumably they grew another in due course. They used to change colour according to their immediate surroundings, and in a matter of seconds they could change from bright blue to brown or red or green. It was fascinating to watch them.

There were other less pleasant creatures, such as scorpions of two varieties: large black ones about 4ins long, horrible looking things which made people really ill on the rare occasions when they were stung, and smaller brown ones which could be extremely painful as I know from experience, but which were not dangerous.

Then there were enormous centipedes up to 7 or 8ins long and as broad as one's finger. They had a set of about ten legs on each side in the front end of their bodies and very poisonous stings which could be excruciatingly painful as well as dangerous. These lived under stones or logs and in holes in banks, and one always looked carefully for both centipedes and scorpions before sitting down.

Snakes were very common and ranged from pythons 12ft long to little vivid green bamboo snakes a foot long. The most dangerous were cobras, of which quite a number were seen and usually killed. It is rather an astonishing fact that out of the thousands of PoWs living and working in the jungle I never heard of a case of anyone being bitten by a poisonous snake or, for that matter, by any other kind.

Chapter 7

Promotion and Reorganization

Throughout the latter part of February and March I continued to convalesce, doing nothing strenuous and having a daily bathe in the river which was very pleasant and almost like a hot bath. We were now in the middle of the dry season and the river was quite shallow. It had a lovely pebbly bottom on which the one could sit with one's head out of the water, and many an hour was spent there by hundreds of those who were convalescent or semi-fit. Even in these early days there were no really fit men, though the term 'fit' was used to cover those who were in reasonable health.

One day, we had to listen to one of Colonel Yanagida's absurd speeches, which he delivered periodically to the whole camp, standing on a table, closing his eyes in thought and uttering short barks and gurgles, completely unintelligible to us since it was delivered in Japanese. It was very difficult not to laugh, though most unwise to do so. Adachi, also standing on the table, would then translate into indifferent English. This particular speech was to thank us for our 'co-operation' in building the railway, regretting the 'hardships we had undergone' and hoping we would again 'co-operate' in more construction higher up the river. Our 'co-operation' to date had led to somewhere about 100 graves and 3,000 very sick men being now in Chungkai camp alone.

Probably owing to the fact that I was a good deal 'below par' I contracted a most irritating kind of skin disease. Tinea, which looks rather like ringworm, attacked large numbers of us. It took months to get rid of it, but I succeeded finally through the help of a Siamese whom I met on a buffalo-buying expedition. He looked at it, brought me a little tin of ointment and indicated that I should rub it on. I did so, quite shortly afterwards was cured and never had it again.

On 30 March 1943 the Japanese committed one of those diabolical crimes which caused us to despise and loathe them with a lasting hatred that will remain with us for the rest of our lives.

On the 29th, the four escaped prisoners who had been recaptured some time earlier were brought up to Chungkai. They were tied up to posts at the guardroom, where they remained stood for most of the day. On seeing them there, Colonel Williamson, the Camp Commandant, went to Yanagida and pleaded for their release or, when that was refused, for some amelioration in their treatment. But he was told not to interfere, that they would have a good evening meal and would soon be all right. They were given a good meal, I believe, and were allowed to lie down after dark.

Next morning, just after daybreak as most of us were getting up, suddenly the comparative quiet of the jungle was broken by a ragged fusillade of about twenty shots. There was complete silence over the camp, and one was conscious only of a quickened heartbeat and sense of tragedy.

The silence was broken by a low growl of curses and blasphemy from the throats of three thousand men. Everyone knew what it meant. Those treacherous, lying, sadistic, yellow devils had murdered four gallant British soldiers in cold blood. A white heat of fury spread through the camp, but it was impotent fury. What could we do? All of us sick men by ordinary standards, most of us so sick as to be incapable of marching ten miles. Disarmed, lacking clothing or adequate food, surrounded by armed troops, and a thousand miles of the worst jungle in the world between us and our own people. There was just nothing we could do except silently express our loathing and disgust, and that we did to the full.

By this time I was really beginning to feel a lot fitter and managed to get out of the camp several times with another officer and a Thai-speaking British corporal to go on water buffalo-buying expeditions. The Japs had given us permission to buy them from the Thais for meat for the camp. The first opportunity we had, we went to see what had been done with the four men who had been shot. We found the place easily enough: a small clearing with four graves in it. No crosses or marks of identification, just four graves in a row and, carelessly thrown among the bushes, four big bamboo structures to which the men had obviously been tied before being shot. Later we got the rough details of the story from local Thais of how these men had been led out here carrying picks and spades, had been made to dig their own graves and then had been shot beside them.

Later, some of us were able to tidy up their graves, make a little enclosure round them and put unnamed crosses up, and after this we took the

Australian padre Thompson out there and held a short service of consecration. All this was unseen by the Japanese. They must have known what we had done, but for the time being we were not prevented.

More men began to pour into the camp from up-country working camps in all stages of sickness, and the overworked MOs and their staff strove heroically to compete against impossible odds.

Early in April, Colonel Williamson and his camp staff were ordered to accompany Colonel Yanagida and a skeleton staff of Japs to open up Takanun Camp about 200km up the railway, and on his departure he appointed Colonel Sainter of the Indian Army to command Chungkai.

I took on the job of Treasurer of hospital funds, which were raised by making a levy on the pay of all officers so that we could buy fruit, eggs and anything else of nutritional value from the canteen or from the Thais who sold round about the camp. Our numbers increased to about 6,000 and the running of the camp and hospital become more and more difficult and exacting.

There was a very low moral code in operation, and theft was rife. No man dared to leave blankets or clothing out to dry unguarded; if he did, the chances were that they would be stolen, taken out by night or even by day, and sold to the Thais who were only too willing to trade in this black market. Nothing was safe from an ever increasing number of thieves, who fattened on the profits of their ill-gotten gains, to the detriment of their fellows.

You may be horrified that British soldiers could descend to such depths, but it must be borne in mind that all of us were up against it and it was a case of the survival of the fittest. No one knew how long it might be before we were released, and life is very dear. There were men drawn into the Army from all grades of life, some of them doubtless from lives of crime at home and from homes where honour had little place. Any man of weak character was liable to be influenced by the temptation now placed before him, knowing that his only chance of life lay in more and better food, and food cost money.

Colonel Sainter appointed an ex-commando officer as Provost Marshal and told him to pick his police carefully and take the necessary steps to combat the crime wave; but commando tactics were not the right method, and there were complaints of severe manhandling by the police and the PM on more than one occasion. This was the cause of several battles of words between Colonel Sainter and me, as some of the victims were men in my battalion. His intentions were right, but I didn't agree with the method.

Early in May there was terrific excitement throughout the camp when the first batch of letters from home arrived. Unfortunately for us, it was then discovered that the officers' letters were not among them, and we had to wait another week for ours. Nevertheless, the knowledge that they were on the way and that the ORs had actually received theirs was a great tonic to everyone. Then on 14 May the officers' letters actually did arrive. I remember the excitement with which I saw the pile of eleven for me. There were four from my wife, six from the children and one from my father. True, they were written more than a year before, but we all felt just as if they were yesterday's news and we all read and re-read them and swapped items of general news and then read them again and felt we really were in touch with home at last. Our whole outlook seemed brighter, and we agreed the war couldn't possibly last more than another year.

Unfortunately, there were many who didn't get letters either then or later, probably due to the inefficiency of the Japanese who, though they revelled in nominal rolls with every conceivable detail of the individual's rank, unit, civilian profession and many other facts, seemed quite incapable of making use of them with accuracy, with results such as the non-delivery of mail to many hundreds of people. When a man died, they were most insistent that all his personal belongings should be handed in to their office with his name and full particulars. Everything was to be sent back to Tokyo to be returned to his relatives, but I never heard of anything being received in this country either during or after the war.

After this, life continued much as usual for a time: men died daily in hospital, averaging more than one a day, and the little cemetery we had planned six months before became almost full. Men who were reasonably strong were sent upriver to add their efforts to those of the thousands already working like slaves in the forward camps along the railway; and for every man who went up, at least one was sent down to Chungkai emaciated and haggard beyond description, to be put in the bamboo huts which were graced by the name of hospital, where heroic doctors strove day and night with little or no medical aids to bring back health to human wrecks.

Suddenly, I was sent for by Colonel Sainter at 2.30 on the afternoon of 24 June. He told me that he and his camp staff were under orders to move to another camp at 6.00 pm and that he proposed to appoint me as Camp Commandant. This was typical of the Japs, who never gave more than the barest minimum of warning of a move, however involved it might be. As I didn't know whether the Japs would approve his selection, I awaited their decision with interest. However, Osata sent for me the next day and said he was sure I would make a good job of it, or words to that effect. I had known Osata for a year now, had always found him very reasonable and knew he was quite well disposed to me after the incident with the maps.

This was the beginning of the most interesting, if most difficult and exacting, period of my PoW existence. I took stock of the situation. There were approximately 5,000 in camp including about 200 officers. It was odd to think that the most responsible command I had had was to be given me as a PoW under these Gilbertian conditions!

My first job was to select my staff. I chose Captain Owen Jenkins of the Dogras as Camp Adjutant, and throughout the next two years he was quite invaluable. No hours were too long for him, and his tact with the Japs and his thoughtfulness and efficiency were magnificent. He was quite the most efficient officer I have had under my command, and many thousands of PoWs should be grateful for his work on their behalf and for his successful efforts in hoodwinking the Japs on numerous occasions to the benefit of the camp.

My next job was to summon the ex-Commando PM and tell him that I felt that he and I would not get on together. In his place I appointed a Scotsman, Lieutenant Robin Calderwood, Inspector in the Malayan Police in Kuala Lumpur in civilian life, and told him to comb out the police force and return any he wished to ordinary duty. I laid down a code of procedure based on King's Regulations as far as possible and told him I wanted crime stamped out in the camp. I promoted him to the local rank of captain and asked him to select an assistant and submit him for my approval. He chose Lieutenant Bill Peck, a burly young subaltern in the Beds & Herts Regiment, in pre-war days a constable in the Metropolitan Police. Bill was the perfect policeman. He had enormous feet and hands, a slow, deep, rumbling voice and a stolid disposition. One could almost see him producing a notebook, licking the pencil and taking down the details of a charge in a London street. He, too, was excellent throughout. There will be more to say later about the exploits of these two in the next two years.

It seemed to me that the organization necessary for my job was almost that of a brigade, and the next problem was to find a good brigade major. Lawrence Pilling, the Second in Command of 135 Bd. Regt. had come up to Chungkai some months previously and was still here. He and I were old friends. We were at school together at Shrewsbury and members of the same club in Manchester in pre-war days. He was always efficient and hard-working, and I decided that I could find no better man for the job; besides, I wanted someone with whom I could discuss all sorts of problems from time to time.

Other posts were filled by carefully selected officers known to Lawrence and Owen Jenkins and me, and gradually we built up a team whose efficiency, loyalty and companionship would have been hard to beat.

One of the most important jobs was that of British Camp Quartermaster, and for that we chose 'Daddy' Marsh, a major in one of the Malayan Volunteer Forces. He was a man well into his fifties with a son (Major Jack Marsh) also a PoW in another camp upriver. 'Daddy' Marsh had a lifetime's experience of dealing with Orientals, having owned an apparently flourishing car dealing business in Shanghai in peacetime. He proved excellent at getting the most out of the Japs that anyone could hope to.

I had too much to do in running the camp to keep on the job of Hospital Treasurer, so I handed that over to Colonel Dean and acted as Chairman of the Hospital Committee. We used to meet once a week and discuss policy and finance with the OC Hospital (at that time Colonel Barrett).

I also found that it was impossible to continue my buffalo-buying expeditions, which I was sorry to give up as it was lovely to get away from the camp into temporary freedom, although I did get out occasionally. I appointed an Indian Army major of mature years, but he came home one day very much the worse for wear in consequence of having sampled the local 'hooch' unwisely and too well while at a *kampong*. I therefore removed him, much to his distress, and appointed Captain Bill Adams, who spoke Thai fluently, having been the head of Shell in Bangkok up to the outbreak of war.

Chapter 8

Boon Pong

We had another Thai-speaking expert in Corporal Johnson of the Federated Malay States Volunteer Forces, who had been officially appointed Thai interpreter by the Japs. Johnson came to me one day and told me he had got a line of communication, through a Thai merchant in Kanburi named Boon Pong, with the European civil internees in Bangkok, who in turn were in touch with certain pro-Allied Thais. He showed me a note saying that we could have money and medical supplies in considerable quantity if I would write a letter undertaking to approach the British Government after the war for repayment. I wrote the necessary letter, and shortly afterwards Johnson came to me one day with 10,000 Thai dollars in notes. I must say that I was not only delighted to have the money for the hospital, but also to know that my letter had got through safely. Had it fallen into Jap hands, I might not have been writing this today.

So much is owed by all of us to Boon Pong for his loyal friendship and help throughout the next two years we spent in Siam that this story would be incomplete without some record of his loyalty to all PoWs and of his gallantry in the face of constant danger from the Japanese invaders of his country.

Boon Pong was a Siamese with possibly some Chinese blood in his ancestry. He owned a prosperous general store in Kanburi and had an interest in the motor haulage business and various other commercial enterprises in that part of Siam. He succeeded in persuading the Japanese to allow him to offer supplies for our canteen soon after our arrival at Chungkai, and these he brought up by motor boat in person or sent up sometimes in charge of his wife or daughter.

From the outset, he made it clear to those of us with whom he came in contact that he had no love for the Japanese and was anxious to do all he could to ameliorate our conditions, quite apart from any question of personal gain from an increase in his trade. It was not long before certain of our own people who spoke fluent Thai – among whom was Corporal Johnson – were able to satisfy themselves that here we had a loyal friend who was prepared to take great risks on our behalf.

In this manner the chain of communication was forged by which we regularly obtained a sum of 5,000 Thai dollars per month for the best part of the ensuing two years. It was handed to me at first by Johnson and later by Bill Adams in rolls of notes which I used to 'bank' in a hollow upright bamboo pole in my quarters. It remained immune during searches by the Japanese camp guards or military police (*Kempeitai*) on several occasions.

Boon Pong was known and trusted by a number of European internees in Bangkok who, in spite of their situation, were able to obtain considerable sums of money and to maintain valuable contacts with the Siamese merchants in that city. As time went on, not only did he establish this contact with us at Chungkai but also with all the other camps formed during the construction of the railway. In addition to money, he sent up supplies of drugs and medicines, much of it at his own expense.

All of this was carried out under the noses of the Japanese and at very great personal risk. On at least two occasions during these years, his premises were searched by the *Kempeitai*, who had become suspicious of his friendly attitude towards the British, but they were unable to prove anything against him.

He maintained contact throughout the whole time we were in Siam, and when the Japanese finally capitulated, he immediately supplied every requirement he was able to, entirely on credit and amounting to thousands of dollars in value. He even went further and advanced many more thousands of dollars in cash simply on the promise of repayment after our release.

Had he been British, it might have been more easily understandable, but from a Siamese it was a wonderful demonstration of trust and friendship. On our release, we took every care to make sure that our debts in cash were repaid, and many of us in our official reports requested our Government to make suitable acknowledgement of the immense debt we all owed to him for his help in a time of great hardship and suffering.

It was a matter of some satisfaction to us that in due course he was awarded the King's Medal for Courage, but in our hearts will always remain a far greater sense of gratitude to that brave and loyal friend than any material acknowledgement could ever express.

Chapter 9

Cholera Breaks out

This great addition to our resources meant a lot more food in the form of meat, eggs, fruit, tinned milk and tinned fish for the hospital. Fortunately, the Japs had at this time no means of checking up on our financial resources, so they didn't realize we were spending much more than usual.

The MOs said they needed milk for many cases, so we instituted a small party of officers to go out daily and buy milk from the owner of a herd of cattle, with Jap permission of course.

After a time, Johnson's line of contact became difficult owing to suspicion on the part of the Japs somewhere in the chain; but in the meantime Bill Adams had established similar contacts through another line, although somehow Boon Pong was still the vital link in the background between Bangkok and us, and the money was delivered to Adams by the head of the Chinese canteen which the Japs had themselves established in the camp.

There seemed to be a noticeable improvement in the demeanour of the Japanese for some considerable time after I took over the camp. I think this was due to the fact that they realized we had a team who were out to improve the camp and run it perhaps rather more efficiently than previously; at any rate, the rations became better and there were fewer 'incidents' with the Japs.

In addition to the Chinese canteen, we had just begun one of our own before I took over. We now enlarged this and extended its activities considerably. The officer in charge was in business of a similar kind in Singapore in peacetime and knew his job from A to Z. He made a first class job of it, and the whole affair reflected the greatest credit on him and his staff, who ultimately numbered about seventy. If I remember rightly, the turn-over got up to 100,000 *ticals* (Thai dollars) a month, and the profit margin was about 15 per cent. The whole of the profits were divided between the hospital and the men's messing in the rest of the camp, with a small sum allocated each month to a special fund administered by me which I could devote as I thought fit to any purpose for the benefit of the camp. With this I bought musical instruments, footballs and sports gear of one sort and another through the Jap QM, who used to go to Bangkok each month and was really helpful.

We still deducted 10 *ticals* per month from all officers' pay and this too went into the General Hospital Funds, so it became quite a large financial undertaking. Of course, all this time more and more very sick men were coming back to us from upriver camps, and our numbers were constantly growing. Furthermore, inflation had started and prices were going up rapidly. Most things had gone up 100 per cent in the last year, so there was always the need for a lot of money.

During July, cholera broke out and cast a certain amount of alarm and despondency over the camp. Several men died in a matter of hours, and the Japs became really alarmed – not for our safety so much as their own, but they produced anti-vaccine and we had a spate of injections for a fortnight, during which the whole camp was 'jabbed' twice each with cholera and dysentery vaccine, and then once against plague. We issued still more strict orders about the boiling of all water for drinking purposes, swimming in the river was stopped for a time and war was made against flies throughout the camp.

About a dozen people died of cholera in the camp before we got the outbreak under control. The cholera cases were isolated in a separate enclosure in tents. There were no special or adequate methods of treating them, but the doctors started a Heath Robinson plant for distilling water, with which they gave saline injections, and in many cases this proved successful. The distillery consisted of a 4-gallon petrol tin over a wood fire tended by two officers all day and producing steam, which was condensed through a series of rubber and tin tubes into big bottles. The plant produced about four gallons per day.

Some, in fact most of, the cases coming down to us from upriver camps were in an appalling condition. Many men literally arrived at Chungkai to die, and the death rate mounted month by month. In June 1943 124 men died and were buried in the second and larger cemetery we had found it necessary to make.

In order to safeguard the camp, and on the OC Hospital's recommendation, we cremated all cholera deaths. It seemed a gruesome business, but common sense dictated the necessity and we tried to carry out the procedure as decently and reverently as possible. Pits were dug in a corner of the camp and funeral pyres made of dry bamboo. The emaciated corpses were soon consumed in the fierce heat, and then some of the ashes were collected in small tins and reverently interred in the cemetery. I had to keep changing the teams of officers and men on this job, which was not surprising. I went down once or twice to the 'crematorium', not because I wanted to but because I felt that I ought to be conversant with any job I asked other men to do.

In between times, there were always unexpected things happening which helped us to keep our reason and sense of humour. As an example, Osata sent for me one day, announced his intention of giving a dinner party and asked me to supply him with a list of guests he ought to invite. As my relations with him had never been unpleasant, and it was obviously meant sincerely, I supplied a list and he produced a most excellent dinner for about twenty senior members of the camp staff. It sounds rather incredible, with men dying daily around us, but the whole situation was so incomprehensible to Western ideas that we came to consider this sort of occasion as nothing out of the ordinary.

Another time, when there was rather a 'blitz' going on and relations were somewhat more strained than usual between us and our captors, they demanded a working party to unload barges at night. At about midnight, when the men had finished the job, the Japs produced a three-egg omelette for each of the 95 men.

Many of the Korean guards had their own views about the Japanese, and after a display of temper by a Japanese sergeant, one Korean waited until the sergeant was out of earshot and then remarked to the British soldiers, 'Jappon Sergeant no flipping good'.

The cookhouse fires consumed vast quantities of wood, and one of our necessary organizations was the camp wood party. This consisted of three officers and about thirty men picked from among the fittest. They had one of the best jobs in camp, going out daily into the jungle to fell trees and carry logs into camp. They fed well, worked hard and were left in peace by the Japs, and there was much competition for the job. With the exception of recurrent attacks of malaria, these men kept very fit. That lasted for over a year, though of course ultimately other arrangements came into force and our wood party had to be discontinued; but it was good while it lasted.

The majority of the more important jobs of work done by officers were carried out by Territorials, which was only to be expected as they had their men to look after, whereas many of the Indian Army officers had no such inducement. Also, many of the latter were senior and less fitted for the tasks. Even if they did no work, however, they were pleasant and sometimes amusing. There were two very 'Poona-Poona' colonels who never did a hand's turn. One of them talked of nothing but hunting and shooting and drawing room conquests; the other hardly ever spoke. The latter developed an abscess on the first finger of his right hand and there was talk of amputating it. His friend's comment in his slow drawly voice was, 'Well, it won't matter much because — doesn't shoot.'

On another occasion one of them was involved in an altercation with a Jap over the contents of a truck. The Jap kept repeating the word 'wire'. At last someone suggested that what the Jap wanted was some wire to be unloaded. 'Well', said the Poona colonel, 'If he means waar, why doesn't he say waar?'

Chapter 10

Adventures of the 'Canary'

During all this time two intrepid young men, Captain Max Webber and his younger brother Donald, both working in Malaya before the war, one in forestry and the other on a rubber estate, had been operating a wireless set in the camp. They were assisted by an ex-BBC engineer, Tom Douglas, who helped to make our set and several others which were taken upriver to other camps.

No praise is too high for these men, who night after night listened in to the news, which was later passed on to the camp. As Camp Commandant I was in their confidence, and they consulted me on all matters appertaining to it. Even before I became Commandant, I was 'in the know', and they used to come to my bunk in the officers' hut and talk over various problems that arose from time to time, such as the indiscretion of some of the more thoughtless officers, who would talk about what they had heard without any thought as to whether a Jap sentry might be within earshot (many of them by this time had acquired a fair knowledge of English), or to discuss how they could arrange to get spare parts and batteries for the 'Canary', as it was called when we talked about it.

The Webber brothers had a small and select band of friends who used to mount guard for them whenever they were 'operating' or doing maintenance work on the 'Canary'. One would see perhaps two of these friends sitting apparently chatting about nothing in particular not far from the Webber hut, but their occupation in reality was keeping watch for Japs.

When the set had to be operated at night or some repair work became necessary after dark, they had one or two nasty moments with the Jap sentries or others off duty coming round unexpectedly – the latter usually bent on doing a financial deal with some officer over a watch or ring.

Quite early on at Chungkai, I remember one such occasion. The Webbers had built themselves a little lean-to shack alongside the main hut, which was very overcrowded. Many of us had done the same, since at this time the Japs put no restriction on our private enterprises so long as we used second-hand materials and didn't pinch new bamboo or *attap* palm roofing sheets. On this particular evening, after dark, he and Donald were doing some repair job to the set and his 'watchdogs' were sitting outside. The set was on the bamboo bed when suddenly there was a warning from the watchdogs. Instantly, a blanket was thrown over the set and the brothers remained sitting on the bed. No sooner had the set been covered than in walked the Korean who usually took the anti-malaria party out, to give some instructions for the next day (Max Webber was one of the anti-malaria party which went out every day to pour oil on pools where mosquitoes would breed near the camp). The guard sat on the bed, resting his hand on the set which was concealed by the blanket and remaining there for several minutes, at the end of which he got up and walked out.

When out of use, the set was buried in a tin box under the brothers' beds, but after a time it was decided that there might be a more thorough search one day, since in one or two of their searches the Japs had taken to prodding the ground here and there, so the Canary was moved.

Don Webber found a job with the blood transfusion centre in the hospital and took the Canary to live in the little hut in which he and one or two others lived next to the centre. It remained here for a considerable time, until we began to feel that if it ever was discovered it might bring serious repercussions down on the whole hospital, which enjoyed singular freedom from Jap intrusion and interference.

Its next home was a large clump of bamboos and bushes quite close to Camp HQ, where I lived with my staff. Here it stayed for many months buried in a box let into the ground, and thither the brothers repaired nightly to take the 8 o'clock news bulletin from New Delhi or San Francisco. All was well there until the Japs decided that the camp would be better without the clump of bushes. They told Camp HQ a short while beforehand that they wished us to cut the clump down, so we were able to warn the Webbers about it.

The next home for it was very ingenious. We had by this time found it necessary to make a new and larger cemetery, and a party of older officers were allowed to act as permanent gardeners – very lovely they made it, but more about that later on. In order to make some sort of shelter near their work they had built a small affair like a summerhouse with its back to a thick clump of bushes. They were brought into the plan and proceeded to build a small extension to the back of the summerhouse, taking care not to let any Japs see them doing it. From the front or sides there was nothing to be seen, but when it was finished there was an extension just big enough for Max and Don to creep into, dig up the set and take the news lying flat on the ground.

It might have been noticed if the same two had walked into the cemetery at the same time every evening, but very fortunately the RC padre had initiated daily Benediction in a secluded part of the cemetery. He was asked to make a slight alteration in the time of the service, and for the next few months our two Scotch Presbyterians became devout Roman Catholics and joined the congregation on its way to and from Benediction, though strangely they were never present during the service!

In later months, once again their mania for clearing the camp caused the Japs to order these bushes to be removed, and a new hiding place had to be found. This time the plan was even bolder, and probably by its very boldness in some ways safer.

The Canary was taken to the Camp Quartermaster's store, in which he kept tools and certain rations, and once again was buried. A thick board was placed over the hole and over this a layer of dry earth. When the set was in operation the officer in charge (Major Pycock) would sit outside reading. The store had a convenient back door through which the staff could enter from their quarters, but the front door was kept locked. On two occasions to my knowledge, Koreans from the Jap 'Q' department came at ill-chosen moments to ask for something from the store, but our party had prepared for such an emergency. In a loud voice, the QM shouted for one of his staff and told him to fetch the key. The staff were well drilled and took a considerable time to fetch it. During this time the QM would carry on a running conversation in Anglo-Japanese, and by the time the key arrived Don and Max had had time to bury the Canary, smooth the ground over and do a quiet and speedy exit through the back door.

For two and a half years these intrepid young Scots provided us with our only link with the outside world, and what an invaluable service it was. We were cut off from every civilized contact, had no newspapers, letters about twice a year and then 12 to 18 months old; without our wireless bulletins we should have been reduced to despair and insanity. But as time went on and we heard first of our successes in North Africa, then Sicily and Italy, and finally about D-Day, the morale and spirit of hope rose higher and higher, and it mattered little what devilry and privations the Japs devised to break our spirits, because we knew that victory lay ahead and that the day would come when our nightmare existence would be over.

During the two years I was Commandant of Chungkai I was in close touch with all that went on, and Max and Donald would consult me about methods of distributing the news. Several times we found it necessary to revise the method when thoughtless individuals – of whom there were a surprising number – became careless. Once or twice we stopped the dissemination of news for a couple of weeks to bring it home to them.

The ultimate and most satisfactory way of spreading it was for a small number of officers to receive it verbally from Max and Donald; they in turn passed it verbally and unostentatiously to small groups in their huts. Strict orders were issued that nothing was to be written – this after one foolish officer had been caught unawares, by a normally fairly astute Korean office clerk called Osawa, reading a closely written sheet of news. This time, however, Osawa was fortunately less astute than usual. He seized the paper, held it upside down, looked at it intently and then handed it back. A number of us were somewhat shaken by this incident, which showed how much more careful we had to be.

On various occasions the Japs instituted what were intended to be snap searches to catch us unawares. Sometimes these were carried out by the camp staff, but several times the *Kempeitai* (military police) organized them. These were always rather unpleasant ordeals for all of us, and more so for those who had anything to worry about.

As time went on and my camp HQ staff and I had daily dealings with the same lot of Korean guards and office clerks for months on end, we found a limited number who really became quite friendly in their curious way; one or two in particular would always come wandering into our HQ living quarters and tip us a line about the possibility of a search perhaps that day or the next. Of course we took the necessary evading action on every occasion; sometimes the search materialized and sometimes it didn't, but we took no chances whenever they gave us a warning. The searches by the *Kempeitai* were usually sprung on the Koreans as well as on us, though sometimes they would get wind of it and they always came and warned us, because there was no love lost between them.

We gradually built up another warning system through our own camp police which was most effective, but this was not until 1943 and 1944. By that time I had succeeded in getting the Japs to allow me a camp police force of forty under Robin Calderwood and his APM Bill Peck, the ex-Metropolitan Police constable. They were all hand-picked and consisted of the best type of ORs, NCOs and men of various units. Every day, some were detailed to watch the approaches to the camp by land and river, and the moment they saw any unusual looking Japanese arrivals, the news was rushed back to Police HQ and from there to Camp HQ and to the Webber brothers. This system served us all well on more than one occasion.

In consultations with the Webbers on the dissemination of the daily news bulletin we gradually worked out a method which would cover the camp effectively even if the Japs should find out that we knew what was happening in the outside world. We instituted a time-lag of 48 hours in giving news to the officers and a rather longer period to the men. It was not that we distrusted the men, but there were so many of them and not all British at that, but also Dutch and mixed-race Dutch/Indonesians, that it was considered essential for the safety of all concerned to take this precaution. It was far better for the camp as a whole to have continuity of news a week or two late than to run any risk of losing it altogether.

The matter of obtaining spare parts and batteries for our Canary provided another problem, but ways and means were always found of getting over it. The set ran on 36 two-volt electric torch cells soldered together, and these lasted about a month. As I mentioned earlier, Max Webber and some of the wireless fans got themselves (through Camp HQ) put on the anti-malaria party. Every day, they sallied forth with tins, buckets of diesel oil and spades to visit swampy parts of the jungle near the camp where they dug ditches and spread oil on the water to stop mosquitoes breeding. This work was useful and effective, but it also covered other practices, one of which was to meet a very friendly Siamese called Char-ruan, who used to obtain batteries and spare parts and meet Max or one of the others in the jungle. There a financial deal was contracted, and in due course the party would march in at the main gate past the guard of about ten Koreans, with several months' supply of batteries and spare parts lying at the bottom of half empty oil tins.

On other occasions, very highly selected members of the police force would be employed in the same way, since sentries never questioned their comings and goings; but that really belongs to another chapter.

The main thing was that for nearly three years this small band of intrepid adventurers continued to outwit the Japs and to keep up the morale of tens of thousands of their fellow men. It is no exaggeration to say that this service quite literally saved the lives of many men who were otherwise so worn out with illness, overwork and unsuitable food that they had no will to live. The cheering stories of Allied successes in the latter stages of the war undoubtedly revived hope and restored the will to live in many. The doctors were magnificent and so were many of their orderlies, but none deserve greater praise or gratitude than the men who maintained and operated wireless sets at the constant risk of torture and death at the hands of our cruel captors.

Chapter 11

The Pace Hots up

Having digressed over a considerable period in the last chapter, we now go back to July 1943. This was about a month or so after I had taken over command of the camp and had begun to feel that we were making some headway in our efforts to raise both moral and physical standards. Meanwhile, away up on the higher reaches of the river, work continuing at a frenzied pace on the construction of the railway, which roughly followed the course of the Quainoy River for 200km.

Day after day we made demands upon the Japanese for improved conditions, more huts, more food, more medicine and less work. Most of our requests and demands remained unanswered, but by our very persistence we did achieve a certain amount. For instance, we got our British-run canteen going on proper lines, and as time went on it became a veritable emporium, where one could place an order for a hot meal of considerably more appetizing character than our earlier culinary efforts; or one could purchase domestic items such as soap, razor blades, peanuts, fruit, eggs, needles, cotton and many other highly prized necessities of life.

Cookhouses were rebuilt on more commodious lines, and the wood party became an organized affair, with several officers and about fifty men who lived in a compound and made daily excursions into the jungle, where they cut down timber then hauled it back, either on trucks or on their shoulders, and cut it up into logs. Every day, cookhouse fatigue parties drew their day's ration of logs from the dump in addition to sending out small parties of semi-convalescent men to collect dead and dry bamboo for kindling.

Messing officers were appointed for each cookhouse which served about 400 men, and a senior messing officer, in control of the whole of the camp's messing, presided over them.

We felt it was necessary to lay down a disciplinary code for battalion commanders so that there should be co-ordination of the scale of punishments which were given for misdemeanours. A limit was set to the number of days of extra fatigues or detention in the Police Hut which they could award, and any particularly bad case was sent up before me and dealt with in my Camp Office. The COs were extremely co-operative over this procedure, at which they might reasonably have taken exception, but in the general desire to raise and maintain the discipline of the camp they gave me the most loyal support. Sometimes I had to inflict punishment on delinquents which, to anyone who reads this, may appear unduly severe; but it was done with the sole object of saving men from becoming the victims of their degradation and to safeguard the property of the many thousands of honest and courageous fellows, who necessarily had to leave their belongings unattended by day while out working and unguarded at night while they slept.

Had we not kept rigidly to this course, I cannot imagine what the result would have been. Money became the be-all and end-all of life for men who daily saw their friends dying like flies for the want of proper food and clothing. To those who gave way to temptation, the theft of a watch or ring or a blanket meant anything from 25 to 100 dollars easy money. There was a terrific black market to be operated with the local Thais out in the jungle. The camp covered 50 acres, there was only a token bamboo fence to be got through by night and worn paths led to certain rendezvous where the buyers would wait to do their clandestine deals. It was all too easy, and the will to survive overcame all other considerations in many men made of weaker stuff.

Time proved that the line we adopted was right. Honest men showed their appreciation, and a better spirit became evident. When I first took over, few other ranks had much respect for officers and salutes were almost non-existent; but gradually the tone altered, until ultimately it was a rare occurrence for me not to receive a soldierly salute from any man as he passed me. On one occasion, however, discipline was carried to what I felt was the limit of necessity.

Our Headquarters latrine was the usual deep pit covered with a wood and bamboo top, above which one squatted when nature called. Our 'benjo' had a discreet *attap* palm-leaf fence in front, but owing to some misfortune, the fence had fallen down on this particular morning so that there was I – wearing my well known blue and scarlet gunner side-hat – exposed to the full view of any passer-by! As I was thus communing with nature, a private soldier passed and, seeing my well known headgear, gave me a particularly smart salute. The Drill Book doesn't lay down what is the correct form of response in such circumstances!

This reminds me of another amusing incident which happened in an officers' *benjo* (Japanese for latrine; the name became universally used). This particular *benjo* had a bamboo latticed fence in front of it with thin bamboos laced vertically forming a V at the top. It was a brilliant moonlight night and the *benjo* was, as usual, being well patronized. Suddenly the group of squatting officers saw a long, sinuous shape crawling along in the V at the top of the low fence, about three feet from their heads. The exodus was incredibly speedy, and little thought of modesty was observed in the process of flight. However, one courageous officer, holding up his shorts with one hand, attacked the intruder with a heavy piece of bamboo and killed it. It was a six-foot cobra.

In Chungkai Camp we continued to receive vast numbers of emaciated men from the railway construction camps every few days. Often they had been four or five days on the journey, and the majority lay motionless, performing the functions of nature where they lay, many of them with acute dysentery, and all this in a tropical country. The state in which they arrived passes description, and only those of us who witnessed it as I did, not once but scores of times, could possibly visualize to what point the human body can suffer and still survive. I wrote the following paragraph at about this time in my diary:

> 16th August, 1943. More and more fellows keep on arriving – many to die – and they all tell the same story of semi-starvation, of beating up, of the sick being ordered out of bed and being beaten if they didn't work hard enough. These things must come out when we are liberated since they are not just one or two instances, but have happened countless times.

In order to cope with such influxes, the hospital organized reception parties for immediate duty whenever a party arrived, and they almost invariably arrived without warning and in the night.

On the camp administration side we organized stretcher and baggage parties to be similarly available, while the Camp QM, Major Marsh, kept a permanent stock of tea, rice, sugar and eggs on hand, from which the night-duty cooks could always produce a meal within a short time for the worn out and famished travellers. The gratitude they expressed proved how welcome was this little effort to make them feel that at last they had come to a place where somebody cared about them. Never have I seen so much genuine kindliness and so many little acts of thoughtfulness and generosity as were demonstrated daily by men who were themselves in no great shape towards men often total strangers to them but whose lot was still worse. It was this feeling which has, I think, forged a lasting bond which remains to this day among ex-PoWs Far East, to an extent which far exceeds any other tie of friendship I have known.

Another activity which became highly organized was hospital welfare. It took a good deal of thinking out before we got the final answer, because sometimes good intentions conflicted with the doctor's treatment of their patients, but ultimately we evolved a system which worked very satisfactorily.

A number of officers were appointed as Hospital Welfare Officers and, by arrangement with the hospital staff, they took round extra food in the form of eggs, fruit and peanuts, as well as soap, cigarettes, books, etc., and delivered them to patients as recommended by the MOs. The patients thereby received individual attention which the overworked medical staff could never have given them outside of their purely medical care. Men who perhaps had no acquaintances in the camp felt they were being cared for, and it helped many of them enormously.

All this was financed by a monthly grant from camp funds. For my own part, I tried to visit some part of the enormous hospital every day and used to have a word with as many men as I could in the time. I had a small fund for welfare purposes which enabled me to buy cigarettes, so that I could always produce some when I went round. It wasn't very much, but the fellows seemed always so pleased to see one that in its small way I used to feel my visits were of some use in cheering them on their way to recovery. The hard part used to be when talking to fellows for whom one knew there was no hope at all; but one developed a technique even for this which, despite knowing it to be false, was excusable. Unfortunately, one had to employ it far too often.

During the summer and autumn of 1943 the numbers of deaths became appallingly high, as the tempo of work up country was driven on at a frenzied pace by the Jap engineers. In August, September and October 157, 221 and 255 men respectively were buried in our cemetery at Chungkai. On several days we reached a death toll of 15. The total of deaths for the seven months June to December was 1,096.

Shortly after this, the Japs ordered us to rebuild the whole camp and we had to produce about 1,200 men and 100 officers each day on hut construction. All the material arrived by water, the bamboo floated down in the form of huge rafts poled along by Siamese, and the *attap* for roofing brought in barges or towed by motor boats.

I remember thinking one day what a really incredible Gilbertian situation I was in. Here I was, an acting Lieutenant Colonel in charge of 900 officers, 30 of whom were lieutenant colonels senior to me, and about 8,000 other ranks; and endeavouring to run the camp on British lines yet completely subject to the rules and whims of a Japanese Second Lieutenant, three *gunsos* (sergeants) and a handful of Korean privates.

There was no fence round the camp. We could wander out into the jungle, collect wood or just go for a walk, with impunity; yet officially we were not allowed to do so, and anyone making a serious bid to escape was certain of being shot or condemned to a long term in gaol, which meant practically certain death.

The Japanese were driving our men with relentless severity in the camps further up the line during this summer, having been given a deadline for the completion of their railway. The result of this was more and more sick and worn out men than ever before, boatloads and trainloads arriving at Chungkai every few days.

The doctors and hospital staff were worked far beyond their capacity, but continued to battle bravely in their heroic efforts to save life, and in many cases their fine work was rewarded. The sights that one encountered in many of the hospital wards at this time were pitiable and gruesome, and past comprehension unless actually seen.

Chapter 12

A Birthday Party

Enough of the morbid side. I will now tell you about our new Camp HQ, which the Japs instructed us to build in August 1943.

We had previously had very inadequate quarters, and Osata, who had quite good ideas at times, produced another one now. He said that I was to produce plans for a large HQ with a private room for myself. When the plans were drawn he approved them, and we got busy with a large gang of the fitter men. The result was really very good. At one end was the Camp Office, in which a number of bamboo tables were built. This led to the clerical staff's living quarters. The other half was devoted to officers' quarters for me and my immediate staff and consisted of a large room with bamboo beds down each side and a dining table down the centre, something which no other hut in the camp possessed. Separated from this room was a smaller one about 10ft square for me. In it I had my camp bed, which I had managed to stick to through everything, a row of bamboo shelves and a table fixed into the ground on bamboo legs, with a fixed bamboo stool. This seclusion was the most delightful sensation I had experienced. My sanctum was respected not only by my own officers but even by the Japs, who never invaded it without asking permission, except once or twice when the *Kempeitai* searched the camp; but even they weren't very thorough or they might have found a lot to interest them.

I generally used to retire here after lunch and sleep for an hour during the hottest part of the day, and during other times I could have private interviews there whenever I wanted to discuss things. I also invited my friends to play bridge with me in the evenings by the light of a hanging coconut oil lamp which the camp tinsmith made for me. Altogether, my little room was a great joy.

During these months I usually had anything up to 10,000 dollars in Siamese notes in my care from the money we were getting in through underground sources. Whenever we got warning of a search I retired hastily to the *benjo* with my diary, which I tucked into the *attap* roof before emerging and watching my quarters being searched. Otherwise, I shouldn't have been able to write this book with the same amount of detail.

On 8 September 1943 I 'celebrated' my (44th) birthday. I wasn't really expecting to celebrate it at all, but the camp saw to it that I did. As it shows so well the bond of friendship which grew up in Chungkai between all ranks, I quote from my diary of 9 September:

> Once again I have spent my birthday as a PoW in Thailand, and as far as such a thing is possible, I really enjoyed it, thanks to the kindly thoughts and deeds of my friends among all ranks. I didn't realize I had so many before. All sorts of people wished me 'happier times ahead'; all the ORs of HQ staff signed a home-made birthday card; one men's cookhouse sent me a lovely pie, just like a home-made beefsteak pie; and the Dutch cookhouse made me a big birthday cake with an icing top and 'Many Happy Return' and the date on it. We had a 'guest night' in our little mess of seventeen and had three guests and a marvellous menu of five courses beautifully cooked. Our Messing Officer, Lieutenant Marsh, produced an amazingly good imitation of beer made from fermented rice, sugar and other ingredients. We played pontoon until 'lights out' and almost forgot we were PoWs.

All this sounds rather incongruous in the face of what I have already written about food or the lack of it, but by ingenuity, resource and a good deal of self sacrifice on the part of kindly people, there were occasions upon which truly wonderful culinary efforts were produced.

There was a good deal of mental as well as physical effort required in running a camp of this size under these conditions, and probably I had not really thrown off the effects of diphtheria in the early part of the year. Anyway, my heart began to protest mildly and used to flutter and palpitate at odd moments. The CO of the hospital diagnosed it as a touch of cardiac beriberi brought about by these causes and ordered me to rest a good deal; he produced a small supply of Vitamin B tablets which he insisted I should take. I felt rather guilty about this, but it was crudely put to me that I was more useful alive than dead, and I was ordered to swallow the tablets and my scruples.

The beriberi was a nuisance, because if I did much walking about the camp my ankles swelled up and ached, and it prevented the tropical ulcers on them from healing up too; so for a matter of months I used to have a couple of hours lying on my bed during the early afternoon instead of supervising parades and going round the camp. One of the greatest blows was that the MO wouldn't let me do any gardening and I had cultivated a rather nice little garden near Camp HQ, where I grew canna lilies, zinnias, African marigolds and, greatest triumph of all, three cuttings from a red rose bush, which I discovered one day on one of my water buffalo-buying expeditions growing in a native *kampong*.

My garden also had a utility section in which I grew maize, French beans, sweet potatoes, spinach and tomatoes. The first crop of tomatoes I grew would have done credit to a market gardener anywhere. I got some seeds from a friend who had saved them from a tomato he had had down in Singapore. I sowed them in boxes, they came up in about three days and by the end of six weeks they had produced a truly wonderful crop and were the envy of the camp.

It was most disappointing to have to give this up, but it was obviously silly to overtax one's limited resources, so I let it go and transplanted the three rose trees to a bed at the entrance to the cemetery, where two of them manfully withstood the move and in due course produced a number of very sweet-smelling blooms.

On 18 October 1943 a big consignment of mail was released and I got thirteen letters from my family; mostly written just about a year ago, but even so it was wonderful to get them and to hear about one's family. My wife told me in one that she had just received my postcard written in June 1942 saying I was a PoW.

It was a happy day for most of the camp, and one could see the rise in morale and spirits reflected in men's faces and in their behaviour. We hit on a useful means of widening the news contained in our letters. Everyone was asked to hand in any interesting news, the whole lot was then sorted out and a camp news sheet was typed in the office and several copies sent round. It was astonishing how much there was of general interest. We learned who had won the Derby, what sort of a year it was in various parts of the country and all sorts of things about life at home.

On 11 November we observed Armistice Day at 11 o' clock, and it was interesting to note that the Japs stood still too during the two minutes' silence and sounding of the Last Post and Reveille. We had several trumpeters and buglers from infantry regiments in the camp, and for this occasion they were trained by a bandmaster in a remote corner of the camp among the bamboos, which effectively muffled the sound. There were five or six of them, and for the actual day they paraded in front of Camp HQ all turned out in clean shirts, shorts, boots and hose tops, with beautifully polished belts and bugles, and on the words of command sounded the two calls with the two minutes' silence in between. It was most impressive. Later, there was a church service at which I read 'Let us now praise famous men' from *Ecclesiasticus* Chapter 44.

Chapter 13

The Stage

L ife became a good deal easier towards the end of 1943. The railway had been completed and the 'speedo' tactics of the Japanese had ceased. They demanded comparatively few work parties for jobs other than the construction of new huts and local work around the camp, and we benefited greatly in consequence. I encouraged concerts and planned the site for a theatre, and this grew to be one of the great features of our camp. We started with very humble and amateurish entertainments, but once given opportunity and encouragement, talent sprang up quite unexpectedly and we soon had a complete theatre with drop curtains, footlights, dressing rooms, wardrobe masters – and 'mistresses'. The latter produced wonderful creations for the female impersonators.

Musical instruments of various sorts existed in the hands of individuals who now got together and formed a band; one could hardly call it an orchestra at this stage, though later on under the musical direction of Lieutenants Norman Smith and Eric Cliffe it aspired to performances of a quite astounding standard and variety and which would have astonished musical critics at home, could they have heard them. We were fortunate in having a professional producer in Colonel Leo Britt, who had spent a good many years in London and New York in the theatrical world. He was officially recognized by the Japs after a time as producer and was excused other more menial work in order to train and produce our shows. We did a potted version of 'Wonder-Bar' and several light musical shows called 'Café Colette', in one of which I took the part of a red-tabbed and elderly colonel with a penchant for the ladies and was to be seen dining at the Café with a 'vision of loveliness' in the shape of Bobby Spong, then ending my part of the act with an excerpt from one of the better known musical comedies. Poor Bobby Spong was sent to Japan in 1944 and drowned when the Japanese transport was sunk.

We also did several straight plays, among which was 'Night Must Fall', in which I had a part, though in spite of that it was voted the best play done in the camp. Unfortunately, we had great difficulty in putting it on. The theatre was of course an open one, and on three consecutive nights we were rained off during the performance.

The camp loved these shows and used to flock to them in thousands. The Japs also patronized them, and though they couldn't understand the words they liked the music and got a lot of amusement out of seeing us dressed up in every conceivable costume. The 'ladies' especially intrigued them.

One day, I was walking round the cookhouses and one of the cooks asked me if I was taking part in the show that night. I said I was, and he expressed approval, saying, 'We've never had a singing Camp Commandant before!'

By the end of 1944 our theatrical efforts had really attained a remarkably high standard. We had an extensive wardrobe, and coloured lighting worked from the wings; a devoted hand of professional makers-up led by Sergeant Taylor of the Norfolks; stagehands and scenic artists who performed wonders of carpentry and decor with bamboo, fishboxes, soot, brick dust, whitewash and mud for the production of the most realistic and convincing scenery, usually painted on large sheets of woven fibre matting which the Japs used normally for partitioning their living quarters. Added to all this was our orchestra, which grew from one or two accordions to a sixteen-piece ensemble in the course of eighteen months, by which time, in addition to the 'squeezeboxes', it contained 1st and 2nd violins, trumpets, a cello (made by the camp joiner out of fish-boxes and some local hardwood), bass drum (also home-made), all sorts of gadgets usually associated with a trap-drummer and one or two miscellaneous woodwind instruments. The cello was a masterpiece. I don't know what happened to it eventually, but it was worthy of a place in the Imperial War Museum. For strings it had various types of field telephone wire, but in spite of this it produced an extremely mellow tone.

We had to be a bit careful about what we put over on stage as the Japs were always on the lookout for anything detrimental to themselves. Some of them could understand more English than we suspected, and once or twice there were 'incidents'. Naturally, we took particular pleasure in getting a laugh at their expense – and we did get a good many.

The camp had a good laugh at my expense at New Year 1945. The Japs gave us a holiday and Lieutenant Kokobo, the Jap Commandant at the time, ordered me to arrange sports in which our fellows and the Jap soldiers could compete.

It was a blazing hot day, and about 11.00 a.m. Kokobo summoned me and my Dutch interpreter to watch the sports with him. We sat in front of the crowd out on the sports ground and he produced a bottle of Chinese brandy, which we proceeded to drink neat. We got through that without any difficulty, but at the end he asked me to go back to his quarters as he said he wished to offer me hospitality to show his appreciation of the way in which I had run the camp while he been in charge! I had no desire to accept, but to refuse would have been a grave insult and the camp would have suffered in consequence.

We therefore went with him, and to my consternation he produced another bottle and kept urging me to 'level-peg' with him, filling up my glass as often as I emptied it. As the bottle got lower, my hopes of escaping rose higher, but it was not to be. Kokobo suddenly bethought himself of my Brigade Major, Billy Jones of the Gordons, and my Adjutant, Owen Jenkins, and sent for them. When they arrived, another bottle was produced, but this time it was *laow*, the local rice spirit. Drunk 'neat', it has a delayed action of no mean effect!

By this time I was getting to the point where I had to think very hard what I was going to say, and things appeared a bit hazy. Somehow we got through the third bottle and were then, thank goodness, given some very well cooked Japanese stew and some fruit, after which we were able to leave. I hoped for the best, and taking as firm a grip of my senses as possible, fixed my eyes on Camp Headquarters and made for it. My comrades told me I steered a perfectly straight course, which I find hard to believe. However, on arrival, they suggested I should take two aspirins from a bottle I had always kept for emergencies. I sank into a deep sleep immediately, which lasted from about 3.00 pm until 7.00 pm, when considerable concern was felt because I was due to take part in a 'Café Colette' show at 8 o'clock.

Desperate measures were obviously required, and Dr Jimmy Hendry was called to the rescue. He came armed with two precious Benzedrine tablets (his only two), woke me up and ordered me to swallow them. They were most effective, and I was able to appear on the stage even though still a bit 'under the influence'.

By this time, of course, the whole camp knew about my session with Kokobo and they flocked to the show to see what effect it had had on me. I remember receiving terrific applause at my entrance on to the stage. All went well until I missed the cue to say goodbye to the 'lovely' with whom I was dining and make my exit singing 'I'll see you again'! Leo Britt, who was playing the part of the 'Maestro', seeing I had missed my cue, gave me a more direct one, but still having a head full of fumes I ignored that too, much to the delight of the audience. Eventually I did realize the situation and made my exit singing in terrific form. The show was voted a great success!

These were the sorts of incident which made us all laugh and forget for the moment we were prisoners without a hope of freedom in sight. That was the great joy of our theatre: we were able to forget for a couple of hours and let our minds pass through a veil into another world for a time, a world we remembered from happier days.

There were many men who were too ill to visit the theatre, so we hit upon the plan of taking the shows to them instead. Of course we could only do the musical items for them, but once every week the orchestra and the singers paid visits to as many hospital huts as possible, and there was no doubt about the popularity of our efforts.

I often used to wonder whether men lying in a semi-conscious state, sometimes in constant pain, would either appreciate or benefit from the proximity of a jazz band playing dance music of the 1941 era, or hearing myself or some other vocalist singing about 'Bachelors Gay' or vocally protesting our love for blue-eyed maidens with golden hair; but surprisingly, even the worst cases appeared to appreciate our efforts.

The Dutch contingent put on one or two excellent shows entirely on their own, but of course accompanied by the camp orchestra. Their speciality was native dancing. The term 'Dutch' included every hue from pure Hollander to chocolate-coloured Javanese. In the East Indies the colour bar is not observed, and an enormous number of Dutchmen have married Javanese and Balinese women, with the result that there are Dutch subjects there of every colour.

Some of these were extremely graceful in their native dances, and one of them, whose name I forget, was the court dancer to a native prince of the Royal House of Java. He performed really beautiful dances, not unlike Russian ballet. One which particularly impressed me was a dance depicting the adoration of a young man for the lotus flower. A large lotus flower with petals closed was at one side of the stage, beautifully designed and made by Dutch stage carpenters. As the young man danced, the petals slowly opened and there arose from them a devastatingly beautiful damsel. Whereupon the young man fell prostrate in adoration while the flower slowly closed, enfolding the beauteous maiden within its petals as the stage lighting slowly faded to darkness. Perhaps this is not a very poetical description, but the dance really was very beautiful and impressive.

I was rather proud of our theatre on account of the fact that in the early days of my command of the camp I gave great encouragement to the valiantly struggling concert party and suggested that we find a spot in the camp which would lend itself to the design of a theatre. Accordingly, I selected a small, shallow valley near the river bank and outlined my idea of having a stage built on one slope and the auditorium formed on the other. This was acted upon, and gangs of willing volunteers spent hours digging rising tiers of seats for the audience and building up a level platform for the stage. We formed a theatrical committee on which I acted as chairman for the first few meetings; then when the organization got going I handed over to someone with more spare time and greater knowledge of the subject. From that there grew up what became a remarkably well equipped organization.

Unfortunately, I had not realized that when the monsoon broke and the river rose some 20ft, my valley would be flooded and much of our work washed away. In consequence of this, a new theatre was subsequently built in another part of the camp, though even this suffered similarly, though less disastrously, later on. Yet in spite of these vicissitudes and the sudden whims of the Japanese, who would periodically forbid the holding of concerts or entertainments as a reprisal for some alleged misdemeanour in the camp, we enjoyed many hours of first-rate entertainment which would have put to shame a vast number of shows held in civilized surroundings at home.

Chapter 14

Keeping Fit

In the late autumn of 1943, the railway having been completed several months before, the Japs began to sort people out into their proper PoW groups. In the early days, this vast collection of British, Australian and Dutch troops had been allocated by battalions into four groups, each under the control of a Japanese colonel. While the railway was being built and sick men were being sent back to various base camps such as Chungkai, these groups become mixed up considerably and we had men of Nos.1, 2 and 4 groups in our camp. There were at this time 7,800 men in Chungkai, and we began to sort them out into their respective groups, ready to move them when required.

The Japs' plan was to leave Nos.2 and 4 at Chungkai and remove the members of No.1 group, sending Osata with them and giving us a new Camp Commander. I was quite sorry to lose Osata, as he had been very reasonable and I had got on with him quite well, to the benefit of the camp in general.

No.3 group were all Australian and they had started working from the other end of the railway at Moulmein, so we had had no contact with them. When the railway was finished, they were brought down to Tamarkan Camp, about three miles away on the Quainoy river above Kanburi.

In actual fact, no move took place for several months, as usually happened with Japanese plans; then all of a sudden there would be the usual 'speedo' and everything was done in furious haste.

Late in November 1943, quite a lot of medical supplies arrived from Bangkok, organized by the Swiss Consul. It was the first legitimate consignment we had had, and though very limited it was invaluable and put new heart into the doctors, medical orderlies and patients alike.

The senior Medical Officer in charge of the hospital (Colonel St. J. Barratt, a Harley Street neurologist) gave me some rather illuminating figures which I entered in my diary: on 27 October 1943 the Chungkai hospital admitted its 10,000th patient in just over a year; on 30 October the 1,000th death occurred. In the cholera epidemic we lost 28 out of 110 cases, which was really a remarkably low percentage when one realizes that the only remedy was saline injections made with water distilled in 4-gallon petrol tins over a wood fire. Up to the end of November there were 94 leg amputations made necessary by tropical ulcers alone. Skin grafting had been resorted to for some time previously in many cases of tropical ulcers which had been treated successfully but still left huge expanses of raw flesh. I watched several of these graftings being done and saw them progress as the graft took effect.

By way of assisting in the recovery of the very large numbers of men who for one reason or another had lost the use of limbs and muscles, we started a kind of clinic under the able guidance of Lieutenant Harry Collins of the Royal Signals. Collins was a qualified instructor in Physical Training and in consultation with Colonel Barrett and other Medical Officers he organized a series of simple forms of exercises for some of the most needy cases.

So successful were his results that very soon the Remedial Centre, as it was called, became quite a large undertaking; and in due course he added about eight assistants to his staff, some of whom had had either civilian or military training previously. Those who had not had such training quickly acquired considerable skill and did a very fine job, the number of patients growing daily until there were over a hundred men being treated each day. Between October 1943 and May 1944 the Centre treated 639 patients.

Many of these were almost completely immobile when they first attended, from causes such as the after-effects of diphtheria, muscular atrophy, contraction of muscles due to tropical ulcers, rheumatism and general debility. In due course, a very large percentage recovered the use of their limbs and muscles as the result of the careful and painstaking treatment they received. There is no question that Collins and his assistants performed a notable job of inestimable value to a large number of men.

This same young officer took the keenest interest in all sports and games in the camp, and due largely to his initiative, organized games came into being. We started with a scratch game of football between Camp Headquarters staff and the cookhouse staff, these by virtue of their employment being some of the fittest men in the camp. This proved so popular that most of the battalions began to find a team of men fit enough to play short games of about forty minutes, and before long we had established a League of about twenty teams and Collins had a magnificent shield made as a League trophy. I hope that shield was brought home as it certainly was a work of art. The excitement over some of the more vital contests was terrific, and several thousand men would line the ground cheering vociferously for their champions. One of the greatest matches was an 'International' on New Year's Day 1944 when England defeated Scotland 2–1 before a 'gate' estimated at 5,000, or as Collins put it in a subsequent report, 'Everyone in the camp who could move!'

In addition to football, we held several athletics meetings, and on more than one occasion the Japanese asked us to arrange a meeting in which their troops could compete. It was a matter of no little surprise and satisfaction to us when, even in their comparatively unfit state, our fellows proved themselves superior to the Japanese and Koreans in quite a number of contests, particularly sprinting and jumping; while on one occasion our time for a 1½ mile race round the camp perimeter was nearly a minute better than the time put up by the Koreans over the same course in a separate race. In addition to these activities, we held several swimming galas in the river which were very popular and amusing.

All these forms of recreation had great value in raising the morale of the camp and were an important part of our daily life.

Chapter 15

Kokobo's Farm

This brought us to Xmas. Once more, our pious hopes of being free by next Xmas had come to nought! However, work on the railway being finished, we were able to have a much pleasanter time than the previous year. My diary, written on 26 December records:

I have been very much impressed with the great Xmas spirit which has been shown on all sides. Everyone seemed determined to do all he could for those less fortunate than himself. I am sure that it is in great measure due to the fine team spirit among all those who are concerned in the running of the camp. They are a grand lot and I could not ask for a more loyal crowd – both officers and men. I feel that they have set an example which the rest of the camp has instinctively followed.

We started the day with Holy Communion in our Bamboo Church at 8 o'clock, and also celebrated Matins at 11 o'clock.

The best Xmas present came at about 10.30 with an air raid warning when one of our own recce planes flew high over the camp. We felt sure it had come to bring us Xmas greetings from home! After the various denominations had held their services, the rest of the day was spent in eating, drinking and being as merry as possible, with games and a concert in the evening. I spent several hours going round the hospital, talking to as many fellows as possible, and found the poor lads in remarkably good spirits. Everyone seemed determined to make their day as bright as resources would permit.

Most of us put out our family photos round our huts, and I managed to put up a real Xmas card, which had been sent to me in Malaya in 1941 and which I produced with great ceremony each Xmas afterwards. I still have it, with each year written on it. We were still divided into battalions in the camp, and there was a general interchange of Xmas cards between battalion commanders. The cards were hand-drawn by amateur artists and usually depicted Xmassy scenes we remembered but which seemed so far away and unattainable.

The Japs allowed us to buy some extra meat in the form of water buffaloes, and as far as I can remember we killed about four on Xmas Eve. They also gave us a lot of fruit, extra sugar and vegetables, doubtless paid for out of the profit they had made from our rations during the preceding months. Eight thousand men and six hundred and fifty officers were a large family to cook Xmas dinner for, but the cooks, helped by many willing volunteers, produced enormous quantities of good things such as we had not tasted for several years.

We had a race meeting in the afternoon with 'horses' made of painted boards which progressed uncertainly over a hazardous course according to the throws of a huge wooden dice made for the occasion. There was a 'Tote' as well as several 'bookies' – vociferous as their species ever were, and lacking only the umbrellas! A good deal of illicit local Siamese 'hooch' found its way into camp, and though there were a few cases of excessive consumption, most people had merely enough to create a spirit of cheerfulness.

Finally we went to bed, tired but relatively happy.

For New Year we had a pantomime staged by the medical orderlies entitled 'So Tight and the Seven Twerps'. It was really very funny and free from vulgarity, and the numerous topical and good humoured 'cracks' at members of the camp staff and other prominent individuals went down in a big way.

I don't think anything very interesting happened for the next month or so, except that Osata left the camp and his place as Commandant was taken by Lieutenant Kokobo (subsequently hanged after our release!). Kokobo was a curious individual, possessed of a dual personality: he could be friendly and pleasant one minute and fly into a furious rage over the most trivial matter the next. I had constant dealings with him for the ensuing twelve months and saw both sides on frequent occasions. He was reputed to be a brave fighting soldier, and I should think this was probably true, but drink was no doubt the cause of his having got no higher that his present rank at the age of about forty-five, and being now relegated to third-line troops in charge of a PoW camp.

Kokobo was full of bright ideas, in many ways quite genuinely directed towards the improvement of the camp. He ordered the commencement of a big gardening scheme of about 10 acres on some open ground half a mile from the camp and close to the river to which large bodies of men were marched out daily, armed with picks, spades and Chinese *chunkols* to prepare the ground from which the camp was to produce a large part of its vegetable ration. Huts were built there under the shade of a clump of old mango trees for a small permanent staff of Japs and PoWs, and there was always competition to be in on these special parties, as those who were selected usually had a much freer existence than was possible in the main camp, which was naturally subject to restrictions which did not exist outside. Kokobo professed to come of farming stock and he certainly had a very fair knowledge of the subject, though his methods were not altogether in accordance with English farming practice.

From gardening, we extended to ducks and pigs. These were to be fed on the by-products of the gardens, but they also had their proper rations. Elaborate duck pens and shelters were erected on the river bank and several hundred young ducklings were bought from the Siamese. The next step was to make pig pens. This was done by digging moats about 4ft deep, with a high bank on the outside, up which the very agile pigs could not climb. The runs so formed were each about 30yds square, with huts in each run. About thirty sows and several boars made their appearance and took up residence, and *qualis* similar to those in which we cooked our rice were installed in which to cook their food. The pigs seemed to thrive on their diet, which was augmented by all the swill from the camp cookhouses taken down each day for them, and in due course there appeared several litters of little pigs.

Kokobo took great interest and pride in his horticultural and agricultural venture and spent most of the day there. He would quite often take off his shirt and work with the men when he was in a good humour, which was more than any of his predecessors had done, and for this reason he commanded more respect; but woe betide any man, British or Jap, whom he thought was slacking! Many were the shouts of '*Koorah*!' ('Come here, you!') followed by a terrific bash on the side of the face with the flat of his powerful hand. Generally speaking, his administration of this degrading form of punishment was not without cause when looked at from his point of view, and it was up to the men to take no liberties when he was in sight.

Having got his pig farm going, he decided to extend it to cattle, with the idea that we should have our meat bought 'on the hoof' and look after it ourselves

The Owtram family in 1927, Jean and Pat in the pram.

Major Owtram before going to the Far East, 1941.

Newland Hall, the family home.

Cary Owtram in Malaya before the Japanese invasion.

Sketch of Colonel Owtram by a fellow prisoner (a poor likeness, according to Pat).

Letter from the War Office in response to Mrs Owtram's request for information.

Tel. No.: Liverpool Wavertree 4000.

Any further communication on this subject should be addressed to :—

    The Under Secretary of State,
      The War Office,
        The Casualty Branch,
          Blue Coat School,
            Church Road,
              Wavertree,
                Liverpool 15.

and the following number quoted :

    O. S. 516. 0. ....(Casualties)

THE WAR OFFICE,

CASUALTY BRANCH,

BLUE COAT SCHOOL,

CHURCH ROAD,

WAVERTREE,

LIVERPOOL, 15.

8 March, 1942.

Madam,

      With reference to your letter of the 2nd March, 1942, addressed to the Prisoners of War Enquiry Office, Curzon Street House, London, I am directed to inform you that according to the latest information available in this Office your husband, Major H.C. Owtram, Royal Artillery, was serving in Malaya during the hostilities which terminated in the capitulation of Singapore on the 15th February, 1942. Every endeavour is being made through diplomatic and other channels to obtain information concerning him, and it is hoped that he is safe although he may be a Prisoner of War. It will be necessary, however, to post him as "Missing" pending receipt of some definite information. In these circumstances you will, no doubt, realise that it is not, at present, possible to communicate with him.

      Immediately any information is obtained it will be sent to you, and I am to request you to be good enough to notify this Office of any change of your address. Should any news reach you from any other source or should you receive any card or letter from your husband, it will be appreciated if you will at once forward it to this Department.

If your husband is reported a prisoner of war, you will be advised as to despatch of letters & parcels.

      The 2½d stamp enclosed with your letter is returned herewith.

           I am,
              Madam,
                Your obedient Servant,

                    F.A. Hawkins

Mrs. D. Owtram,
  Newland Hall,
  Nr. Lancaster.

Burma-Thailand Railway, *c.*1943. Prisoners of war carrying sleepers in Burma, about 40km south of Thanbyuzayat.

The interior of the hospital hut at Wampo on the Burma-Thailand Railway.

(*L to R*) Jean, Bob and Pat Owtram.
A wartime family Christmas.

(*Below left*) Pat during the war.

Jean in FANY uniform. Cairo, 1944.

The first page of the diary
(Imperial War Museum).

Digging up the diary, 1945.
Photograph taken by the
Swiss consul.

A family group photographed by Jean the day after Colonel Owtram's return from the Far East. (*L to R*) Colonel C.J. Daniel, Bob, Bunty, Cary, Pat and Colonel H.H. Owtram.

Receiving the OBE. (*L to R*) Pat, Cary and Bunty Owtram, Jean.

Colonel Owtram in retirement at Newland Hall.

The Owtrams in the 1950s.

– a very sensible idea in view of the fact that previously all our meat was sent up from Kanburi in open boats in the blazing sunshine and arrived on the verge of putrefaction and covered with hordes of bluebottles. Unfortunately, he omitted to advise me of the imminence of his latest brainwave, and one evening I was told that Kokobo wanted me. I went to his quarters and was informed by the interpreter that we were to have 500 cattle. I expressed my approval and was then told that 100 were on their way. I asked when they would arrive, whereupon the interpreter said 'They come now. You take.'

'What, now? This moment?'

'Yes, you take. I show you.'

This was a bit of a facer. Six o'clock in the evening, with one hour's daylight left, to be presented personally with 100 wild and milling cattle single-handed!

Off we went to one of the camp entrances and there, sure enough, was a herd of Siamese cattle with a villainous looking party of about half a dozen local drovers. Then I had a sudden brainwave. We had a lot of Australians in the camp, and I knew some of them were cattlemen, in particular a very excellent warrant officer; so telling the drover in charge in my very inadequate Siamese that I would fetch men to take charge of the cattle, I went in search of the Australian. Unfortunately, he wasn't to be found, so for the time being I collected a party of volunteers – most of whom knew nothing about cattle – and took them with me. We took over the beasts and drove them on to some open ground outside the camp, and I arranged that the men would mount guard over them during the night.

As I expected, there were about twenty cattle missing in the morning, and we had parties out in the jungle trying to find them for the next two days. We found several, but suspected the local Thais had made the most of such an opportunity and had driven the others off to join their own beasts.

The following morning, I asked the Australian warrant officer if he would select a party of his men to take on the job of looking after our new possessions. They jumped at the idea and did it admirably for many months. It was a very popular job, as they lived outside the camp and led a free existence, which suited them down to the ground. From time to time more cattle arrived, until we had about 250. Quite a lot of calves were born to add to the interest, and I used to go out often to have a look at the herd and see how the men were getting on.

Of course, the object of the cattle ranching exploit was to provide us with meat, so every week a number of the older animals which showed signs of ailing, plus a few of the younger ones, so long as they were not thought to be 'in calf', were driven in to the camp and butchered.

I am afraid the abattoir was pretty crude, but we had no option. We asked the Japanese to let us shoot the beasts, but they said ammunition was too precious! About ten rounds a week would have sufficed, so that was a poor excuse. However, since they would give use no rifles and ammunition and would not shoot them themselves, we had to kill the poor brutes with a sledgehammer. As a rule this was completely effective with the first blow; it certainly was with the cattle, but with the water buffaloes which we still bought to augment the ration I regret to say that very occasionally it took more than one blow. They had enormously thick skulls and anything less than a well aimed blow in one particular spot at the base of the skull was useless. One man, a blacksmith, by trade and six feet tall, was the regular executioner, and took the greatest care in endeavouring to carry out his unpleasant task as mercifully as possible. It was a case of the buffaloes' lives or ours, through starvation, so it had to be the buffaloes'.

Taking of buffaloes reminds me of a rather humorous incident with a Japanese sergeant, one of the few instances when I ever heard one of our captors make a joke with any sense. Shortly after we first acquired our herd of Siamese cattle, one of the sergeants wanted me to go and count them. Just as we got to where they were grazing, we passed some water buffaloes; the Jap turned to me with a grin and, pointing first at the Siamese cattle and then at the water buffaloes, said in his very broken English, 'Army cows; Navy cows!'

Chapter 16

The White Slug

Having had a succession of quite incompetent and usually incomprehensible Japanese interpreters, we got a new one early this year – Shutaro Matsushita by name – who really was a help. He spoke perfect English – or perhaps perfect American would be nearer the truth, since he had spent 28 years there. It made my job far easier than it had been in the past, as I could go to his quarters and discuss things with him instead of having to think carefully before I said anything, as was the case with his predecessors – and even then as often as not I didn't understand them when they tried to talk English. One of them loved using long words, and his favourite expression was to say to anyone with whom he wanted to discuss something, 'You come my office, I have communications with you.' Needless to say, 'Communications' became his nickname!

I had many discussions with Matsushita about matters concerning the camp and I remember him saying once when I had complained about a case of ill-treatment by Kokobo and his Jap NCOs, 'These people don't understand, they aren't civilized'!

One immediate result of his arrival was that we got a large batch of letters which had been lying in the Japs' office for weeks. They had said they must be censored before we received them but they had no one who could read them, so we just didn't get them. Matsushita made no bones about it; he read about one in ten quickly through and bundled them out to us. I wish he had stayed with us for the rest of our time, but whether he was not sufficiently anti-PoW or not, I do not know, but he was moved after a few months, and for a time there was no Japanese interpreter.

In March 1944 Colonel Williamson and his party arrived back to swell the throng, and for several months we had a strength of 10,500, including 900 officers, of whom 30 were colonels, nearly all senior to me! At about this time the Japanese began to talk of sending large numbers of men by sea to Japan. We were somewhat sceptical about it, having a fair idea – thanks to our wireless news – that the Pacific was becoming an increasingly difficult area for them in which to operate their ships. However, it subsequently proved to be no idle talk.

I was confined to my bed for a few days in April with several tropical ulcers on my ankles which refused to heal up and became rather painful, and during this period Matsushita was transferred elsewhere, but he seemed genuinely sorry to be leaving Chungkai. He had been a great help during his short stay, and he came to say goodbye to me which was friendly.

I remember him being very upset one day when Kokobo fell into one of his rages on account of a fire in one of our cookhouses which caused a certain amount of damage to the *attap* palm roof. Kokobo summoned all the messing officers, had them paraded before him, raved at them in Japanese and then stumped off. I was also summoned to be present. Matsushita then translated the diatribe into suitable English and said that Kokobo had ordered his Quartermaster Sergeant – a horrible specimen called Sakano and nicknamed by us 'the White Slug' – to punish each officer.

As only the messing officer in charge of the cookhouse in question could in any way be held responsible, I was furious and demanded to see Kokobo again, but the White Slug shouted something at me in Japanese and proceeded to hit each of them a welt across the face with his leather belt. I shouted abuse at Sakano and endeavoured to get between him and the next man he was about to hit, at which he pushed me out of his way with more oaths, and Matsushita shouted, 'Stop, Colonel, you'll only make it worse for them.' So I had to stand and watch about fifteen British officers being belted by a sneaking little Japanese sergeant. Matsushita was a white as a sheet and afterwards called me to his room and told me he was disgusted with his own race.

This was not by any means the only occasion on which I had to stand by while officers or men were knocked about. You may wonder why I didn't resort to more physical action when these incidents happened, but we had learned by bitter experience that anyone who resisted was either set upon by the guards with rifle butts, fists and boots, or the unfortunates who were being punished would receive still more than they had already got; sometimes both happened, so it paid best to keep a tight hold on one's temper in my case and for the wretched victims to stand and 'take it'.

From time to time we had a lot of trouble with Korean guards hitting PoWs with sticks. I invariably protested to the Japanese Camp Commander as forcibly as I could whenever this happened, and on several occasions during Kokobo's reign he investigated my allegations, had the Korean concerned up in front of him and cursed him in Japanese; several times we were told he had set about his own men when he was satisfied that they had been at fault. I must give Kokobo his due in that although a rogue and a bully, he had definite ideas of right and wrong and was quite as hard on his own men as on ours. My regular protests usually proved effective, and we would have freedom from 'stick' incidents for a time.

Chapter 17

I Take A Rest

In May 1944 No.4 Group were all moved by barge down river to Tamuan Camp, and about 1,000 of the worst hospital cases, mostly people who were considered unlikely to be out for several months, were moved by train to Nakom Pratom, a newly constructed base hospital nearer Bangkok, where according to the Japanese they would receive every medical attention. We had heard these tales before and took it with a grain of salt; I believe the new hospital did prove to be an improvement in some ways, but the rules and regulations of the Japs in charge were stricter than at Chungkai, and it was less pleasant to live in as a camp.

Earlier in the year, Colonel Barrett was sent to Kanburi to take over part of the hospital at the PoW camp, and an Australian, Colonel E. E. Dunlop, came to run our hospital. He was magnificent. Aged about twenty-nine, he was about 6ft 3ins tall, an athlete and rugger player of no mean ability and a delightful man to work with. The hospital improved no end under his able administration and he made a point of continually badgering the Japs for more medicine, dressings and equipment.

They hated him, principally I think because he was so tall and they were more than ever conscious of their lack of size, which aggravated their inferiority complex; then of course they couldn't really reach high enough to slap his face, and that annoyed them still more. Unfortunately, Dunlop was moved to another camp after being with us for less than a year, and we were all sorry to see him go.

The early summer of 1944 was marked by a noticeable improvement in behaviour by the Japs, who became rather more lenient in their treatment in that they allowed us to expand our canteen facilities, theatrical productions and time allowed for games and sports. The canteen had become a veritable Fortnum & Mason's, where one could obtain most of one's daily requisites as well as complete cooked meals and at one time a shave and haircut; but after a time we divorced the barbers' shop from the canteen and set up a separate establishment under the control of Sergeant Taylor of the Norfolks, who ran it admirably and quite as efficiently as he now runs the hairdressing department of a well known establishment in Piccadilly. The manager of that establishment informed me that business had had a wonderful increase due to the numbers of ex-PoWs who invariably visit Taylor for a haircut when they are in London. I always make a point of doing so myself, and hear news of many old friends while 'Sergeant' Taylor practises his art upon me.

There was an unpleasant incident one day in June 1944 when Major Richardson – our then Camp Quartermaster – had an altercation with a particularly objectionable Korean who was in charge of the loading and unloading of supply barges on the river bank. His real name was Takamoto, but he was nicknamed 'the Admiral' by reason of his employment. Anyway, an argument arose over the unloading of a barge, and Takamoto lost his temper as usual and hit Major Richardson on the face with a heavy stick and broke his jaw, which resulted in his being in hospital for the next month. I took this up with the Japanese Commandant both in writing and verbally, but got virtually no satisfaction out of him, though orders were at least given that officers were not be hit with sticks.

At the end of May 1944 the one and only consignment of American Red Cross parcels arrived, and though they should have averaged one parcel between two men, they only worked out at one between five by the time they reached us, the Japs having taken their 'rake-off' on the way. Still, we were thankful to get anything at all though we cursed the Japs for their dishonesty and disregard for the laws and usages of war. Most of the stuff which could be put to better use in the hospital was sent there. But this still allowed a small collection of luxuries per man all round. It was a wonderful treat to taste cheese, spam, butter, jam and things of that sort which we hadn't seen for years.

Shortly after this, the Japs decided that Colonel Williamson ought to take the camp over again, and ordered him to do so. They said that it was not that they were dissatisfied with my jurisdiction at all, but as they had always regarded him as the senior lieutenant colonel in No.2 Group they wanted him to continue now that he had come back to Chungkai. I handed over the reins to him in early June, and though I was sorry to give up the job in many ways, I was quite ready for a rest and was able to have a much more peaceful time. However, Colonel Williamson retained me as a 'counsellor' and discussed many of his problems with me, so that I was still 'in the picture' but without the responsibility. This arrangement lasted until September, when I was once more called upon to take over from him.

In the meantime, I had come to the conclusion that my diary, which I had written up about once a week for the last 2½ years, was too dangerous an object to have lying about, since the Japs had long ago forbidden the keeping of diaries. I therefore went into consultation with certain officer friends who looked after the cemetery and also with 'Max' Pemberton, who was now OC Hospital and with whom I had travelled out to Singapore in the SS *Dominion Monarch*.

Max produced an enormous bottle capable of holding about a gallon. Into this I inserted my diary and various incriminating letters and papers about Japanese orders and acts of brutality, and sealed the cork with wax collected from the tops of quinine bottles. The bottle was then put into a petrol tin and surreptitiously buried about two feet down in a grave while the patrolling Jap sentry was at the far end of his beat. I borrowed a compass from a friend and took cross bearings from behind some bushes, in addition to making a note of the number of the grave and the occupant's name. These I wrote on the back of my eldest daughter's photograph in such form as would not be recognizable as a compass bearing.

I realized that the chances of being able to recover my diary were remote, but the chances of being able to keep it without discovery were still more remote and the consequences would have been disastrous, so what I did seemed the wisest course.

Chapter 18

'Amputs'

I have written a good deal about the medical side of our troubles, but for the information of anyone who may be particularly interested in the subject I recount a typical operation to show the conditions in which we existed.

One day in August 1943 our leading surgeon – Marcovitch by name, a loquacious and amusing Polish-Canadian with very considerable ability in his profession – asked me to go over to the hospital and watch a leg amputation, as he had had some discussion with the other doctors over a policy he had decided upon, and he wanted me to see one of his operations performed so that, should his policy be criticized after our release, I might be able to give my views if called upon.

There were an enormous number of terrible cases of tropical ulcers at this time, and many men were dying from the consequent poisoning of their systems. Marcovitch contended that amputation of the leg in certain cases would give a much better chance of survival, and I should say from subsequent experience that his contention was right.

I want over to the hospital at the appointed hour and arrived at the 'theatre', the open end of an *attap*-roofed hut; the operating table was the end section of the bug-infested bamboo benches on which men slept. The only contribution supplied by the Japanese medical department was some chloroform; everything else was provided from our own resources. The patient was so emaciated that his body was literally nothing but skin and bone; his thigh, where the amputation was to be performed, was about half as thick as his knee joint.

There were two enormous ulcers on the leg, one extending from just below the knee to some four inches above the ankle, the flesh being eaten away to such a degree that the tibia was exposed for about ten inches. The other had spread over the whole of the inside of his foot, exposing several square inches of the ankle bone.

Several medical orderlies stood by to assist the anaesthetist and the surgeon – all of them clad only in shorts with a sweatband round their forehead to prevent sweat dripping on to the patient.

Marcovitch made his incision on the thigh, all the while supplying a running commentary for the benefit and interest of a small crowd of onlookers. There was practically no flesh to deal with, but he clipped or tied the various arteries as he came to them and then sawed through the bone. There was no proper saw, but the British camp carpenter had supplied his tenon saw, and this had been well boiled before use. By way of antiseptic appliances there were a couple of much chipped enamel bowls of hot water into which permanganate of potash had been put. Swabs and bandages were bits of gauze or other material, stained brown by repeated use on previous occasions.

Whenever a gust of wind blew, little eddies of dust flew through the air, while flies and blue bottles in their hundreds buzzed incessantly round and were flicked off when they settled on the scene of operation. In well under a quarter of an hour the operation was concluded and the patient carried back on a stretcher to his bed of blankets or sacks spread over a bamboo 'spring mattress'. I think I am right in saying that there was no catgut for suturing and that silk was used for the purpose.

This was only one of more than a hundred typical instances where conditions were similar, but the results undoubtedly warranted the operation. I have seen many men lying in constant pain before having their legs off who made immediate progress from that moment – men whose lives were undoubtedly saved thereby. It was a common occurrence for me to find a man in hospital in the afternoon contentedly smoking a cigarette, having had a leg amputated in the morning, and saying how much better he felt in consequence.

When one considers the precautions taken in English hospitals it seems incredible that any of the 'amputs', as we called them, survived. Cases of gangrene or the stumps going septic were virtually nil; possibly the explanation lies in the power of the tropical sun, which may have sterilized the air and thus prevented infection. I don't know. I leave that for those better versed in medical knowledge to explain.

Drastic though the policy may have appeared, the fact remains that a high percentage of these men lived who otherwise must assuredly have succumbed to the gradual and inexorable poisoning of their already weakened systems, and I maintain that the results justified the policy.

The Japanese attitude throughout the years we spent in Siam was that a man unfit for work was a useless drain upon the resources of the Japanese Empire and therefore could better be dispensed with than cared for. Life held no value for them unless it could be calculated in terms of working potential.

There was one notorious case in one of the upriver camps concerning an English soldier who had developed cholera. The Japanese officer in charge ordered a Korean sentry to shoot him. To give the Korean his due, he was unwilling to obey, but fear of the consequences of refusal was greater. Instead of carrying out the order from the shortest possible range, he withdrew some thirty yards and with trembling hands raised the rifle. At this point, one of the British medical men rushed at him and removed his rifle, saying he preferred to shoot the man himself if it had to be done. The patient was dying and unconscious, it was only a matter of hours and there was no hope of recovery. The British soldier carried out the deed instantaneously and humanely.

Reading this in the security of civilization, it may be thought that the British soldier should have refused at all costs, but what would have been the use? The Japs were in command of the situation. The deed would have been carried out by them in any case. They were notoriously bad shots and the patient's suffering would more than probably have been increased. There was a sequel to the affair in that a report of the occurrence reached Japanese Headquarters in Bangkok, and the officer was court-martialled, but the defence succeeded in 'proving' that the man was dead when the officer gave the order; he was exonerated, I think, or at the worst reprimanded.

In Chungkai camp we gave those who died a military funeral, which was carried out with the utmost reverence and respect. There were often funerals in both morning and afternoon, since climatic conditions rendered it imperative to bury men within a few hours of death. The funeral cortèges – sometimes there were as many as six bearer parties at a time in the worst period of 1943 – would form up at the mortuary and, carrying the bodies on bamboo stretchers shoulder high, each draped with the flag of his country, they marched in slow time through the camp to the cemetery, led by the Padre and followed by friends and representatives of each man's regiment.

For many months I made a point of attending all the funerals, but they became so frequent that it was impossible to do this on every occasion; even so, I attended them as often as possible. As the solemn procession passed through the camp men came to attention everywhere and those with hats saluted. On arrival at the cemetery the Padre read a brief service and the bodies were lowered gently and reverently into the graves dug five feet deep in the sandy soil.

As the Blessing ended, the whole party came to attention and buglers sounded the Last Post followed by Reveille. During the Last Post all officers saluted. The calls could be heard back in the camp, and it was the custom there for every officer and man to come to 'attention' no matter what he was doing. Ultimately, the Japanese forbade working parties to stop working, as they considered it a waste of time, but the order was disregarded more often than observed.

In the really beautiful setting of the cemetery, blazing with beds of canna lilies, scarlet hibiscus bushes and other flowers and flowering shrubs, backed by the dark green of the jungle trees, these services lacked nothing in reverence and humility. In fact, one came away with a feeling of something akin to happiness in the knowledge that these men had passed beyond the reach of pain and hunger, and that their earthly remains reposed secure for all time in a place of beauty, for such it most certainly was.

In many cases men from the dead man's regiment would make a wreath of flowers collected from the cemetery or from patches of garden cultivated by themselves, or from the wild flowers of the jungle, and these were laid reverently on the biers. Our cemetery was cared for by a party of about sixteen of the older officers, for whom we obtained exemption from other duties, and they made a lovely job of it. At certain times of the year it was perfectly beautiful, and I would often go and walk round in an evening for the pure joy of the peace and quiet and the beauty of the surroundings.

In the early days crosses were put up by individuals in some cases, but many graves had no crosses. However, we kept a chart and plan in Camp Headquarters, and during 1944, after repeated requests for the necessary wood had been refused, we succeeded at last in obtaining sufficient from the Japanese to provide a cross for every grave. In addition to the individual crosses, I conceived the idea of adding to them by designing a big central cross, and having noticed some derelict poles about 12ft high standing in an open piece of ground outside the camp about a mile away during some of my excursions in search of water buffaloes and other supplies of one sort and another, I took a party of officers out with me and brought two of the longest of these hardwood poles back to camp. The camp carpenters made them into a cross and we erected it in the centre of the cemetery.

When the day of our liberation came I took the Swiss Red Cross representative up to Chungkai and suggested to him how our cemetery might be made into a very beautiful permanent one by opening up the intervening space between it and the river, and he was of the same opinion. It is a matter of great happiness to me that not only has my suggestion been acted upon, but in a photograph of the cemetery as it now is there appears a large plain central cross of similar dimensions to and situated in the exact site of the one I had put up in 1944.

Surrounded by green-clad hills, the perpetual green of the jungle foliage, flowers of every colour which seem to be in bloom nearly the whole year round and with the silent and noble Quainoy river flowing past, those who lie there have a resting place more beautiful than any I know of in England, and though they lie in Siam, those hallowed acres have become a bit of England, which we who lived there and survived can never forget.

Chapter 19

The Lighter Side

And now let me tell you of the lighter side of our life.

There were many funny experiences of one kind and another. I remember talking to a man in hospital one day who asked me where I came from. When I told him, he said he had a friend who lived in those parts, so I told him to ask his friend to come to Camp HQ one evening and have a chat with me. The man didn't come, but I met my hospital friend again some time later and told him so. His reply was that the other man had been too shy to come. 'But,' said my friend, 'I told him he needn't be, because though you was a Colonel you was still a gentleman.'

One day, one of the troops was walking near a gate of the camp seldom used by any of the Japanese officers or NCOs. The Korean guard on sentry duty could speak a fair amount of English. The day was very hot and he had had a late night and was very tired.

'Soldier come here', he called out. 'Me very tired, sleep-o. You take rifle, I sleep-o. If Jappon come you wakey.'

Handing his rifle and bayonet to the astonished soldier, he proceeded to lie down beneath the shade of a tree and went fast asleep, while the British soldier took over the duties of sentry until he saw the relief guard approaching, when he woke his friend and handed him back his rifle!

On another occasion, I had been called into the Japanese officers' quarters to find Lieutenant Kokobo – the Commandant – with four British soldiers before him in charge of Korean guards. They had been caught smuggling in tobacco. Kokobo explained through his interpreter that he proposed to deal out summary justice to them. I knew that meant a pretty unpleasant dose of very hard face-slapping, but there didn't seem much possibility of getting them out of it. The men admitted the charge and told me they knew what they were in for and could take it.

The upshot of the matter was of course that Kokobo administered the punishment with his usual vigour, and it must have hurt like hell, but being sportsmen they took it without a murmur, while I had to watch in silent fury. When it was over, he said I could dismiss them, which I did after expressing my feelings about all Japanese and these in particular (in English!). The lads knew I could do nothing and were even grateful for my futile efforts on their behalf.

When they had gone, Kokobo made signs to me to follow him to his private quarters, and I imagined I was about to receive a lecture through the interpreter. When we got inside his room he sat down, Japanese-fashion, on the floor and signalled to me to sit beside him, then shouted something to a servant, and a bottle of brandy and glasses arrived. He then proceeded to drink my health!

I was not in the mood to respond cordially, which he noticed immediately, burst into a roar of laughter, patted me on the back and then, slapping himself playfully on the cheek, pulled a long face and looked across at me, still roaring with laughter! I had to laugh, too; the whole thing was so completely incongruous.

Poached eggs were then produced for the party, which now consisted of his interpreter and the Japanese sergeant major in addition. They derived much amusement from watching me trying to deal with a lightly poached egg with chopsticks. I wasn't awfully successful, although it seemed to present little difficulty to them.

The aptitude of British troops for finding humour in circumstances of adversity is one of their most priceless possessions, and on numerous occasions it showed itself during our imprisonment at times when life was most uncomfortable. Unfortunately, their wit is often rather crude, but among a large body of men living in primitive conditions as we were, this is not unnatural. At the risk of causing disapproval, I feel I must relate one story which created considerable amusement and illustrates my point.

In the rainy season of 1944, the two rivers which converge below Chungkai rose many feet very suddenly and the low-lying parts of the camp became flooded, the occupants being driven out of many of their huts. We began digging 'bunds' (banks of earth) feverishly to try and save part of the camp, but the rising waters beat us, and I issued a special order that the 'essential services' should all be concentrated on the one and only bit of high ground. Essential services meant latrine pits, cookhouses and urinal pits. This order was circulated quickly round the camp, and hordes of men set to work to carry it out.

Within an hour, this small area was being referred to by the troops as the 'A. R. P. Centre' – 'Arseholes, Rissoles and Pissoles'!

Chapter 20

Chungkai Church

Although I have referred here and there to our church services, the church itself and our religious activities formed such a large and central feature of our existence that I propose to devote a chapter to more detailed description of that side of our life.

Going back to the early days of our captivity, on the way up to Siam by train, I found myself travelling for the last half of our journey in a baggage truck, sitting on a pile of valises with about five officers, among whom was an elderly Australian, well on in his fifties, by the name of Thompson. I didn't realize at the time that this kindly and likeable man was the Revd R. J. Thompson, Canon of Singapore Cathedral and Chaplain to one of the Volunteer Regiments in Malaya. After our arrival in Ban Pong – our first camp in Siam – I got to know him much better.

Our first church services were held in the broken-down end of a dilapidated hut with a floor of stinking mud and pervaded by the overpowering aroma of nearby latrines. An empty crate with a whitish table cloth over it formed the altar, and there we held Holy Communion and also Matins. In spite of the surroundings and conditions, those services were more real and heartening then many I have attended before or since. It became an established custom after that, until we moved up country to Chungkai, to have an outdoor service every Sunday.

When the main body of the camp moved there in September 1942, Padre Thompson elected to remain behind and help to look after those in hospital at Ban Pong, so I didn't meet him again for several months, in fact not until about the time when I was recovering from diphtheria in the spring of 1943. He arrived up at Chungkai looking rather tired and frail, and I invited him to share a little lean-to hut I had built outside the main officers' hut.

Shortly after this, we decided that we ought to build a camp church which had for a long time been the Padre's dearest wish. We obtained materials from the Japs for the purpose and under the guidance of one or two experts in the construction of bamboo building there arose quickly a most attractive church capable of seating something like 100 people. The altar was raised up on a platform of earth edged with split bamboo, the altar itself being made of bamboo and disused fish-boxes obtained from the quartermaster. The altar rails were of bamboo, as were the rather uncomfortable pews, and the roof was made of the usual *attap* palm with a reredos of the same material.

Soon after it was finished, I remember bringing in big bunches of frangipani – the lovely white flowering tree with a strong lemon scent always planted around the local temples – with which we decorated the church for Easter. The effect was really lovely. This soon led to an extension of our horticultural efforts, and the ground all round was cleared of everything except grass, in which hibiscus and other flowering shrubs were planted.

Every Sunday, one of us obtained flowers for the altar, and Holy Communion was celebrated at 7.00 am, then Matins and Evensong in their turn. Sometimes we had a combined non-denominational service, and at others Padre Thompson and the Methodist and Presbyterian padres arranged a timetable so that each denomination could have its own service. The number of officers and men who attended every service would have heartened many a parish priest at home. Religion meant a great deal to us, and I for one was bitterly disappointed if ever I was debarred from attending.

In the days when I was in charge of this large camp, when conditions were at their worst and men were dying in dozens every day, I derived peace of mind and guidance from these services to a far greater extent than I had ever experienced before. We were particularly blessed in Padre Thompson, who was a magnificent example of fortitude and courage throughout and, though he spent his sixtieth birthday as a PoW, survived the whole three and a half years to return to Australia upon our release. I found him a wise counsellor and a loyal friend throughout.

The Roman Catholics had their church also, but there was not always an RC priest in the camp. There were also a number of Jews, and they too had their services, though they had no padre. The camp dentist, Captain Arkush, a very devout Jew and one of the most likeable people in the camp, was the mainspring of their religious devotion. 'Arkie' was a grand fellow, generous and self-sacrificing to a degree, and was held in respect and affection by everyone – and he was a good dentist too!

Sometimes the Korean sentries would come and stand around during our church services and watch, and usually they had the decency to respect the privacy of our devotions even if they couldn't understand them.

All went well until the end of 1944, when the camp was made much smaller and our church was outside the reduced perimeter. When all officers were moved to Kanburi Camp we were in the process of building another church, but I never saw it completed. However, it could never have been as picturesque as our first attempt, set in a green clearing amid the jungle trees and clumps of evergreen bamboo, where it was possible to escape from the noisy turmoil of the camp to an oasis of peace and quiet.

Most of the camps held services when they could, and some of the larger ones built churches, but I believe none had a church of such a permanent and perfect design as ours.

Chapter 21

The Cemetery

Soon after we had arrived at Chungkai from Ban Pong in the autumn of 1942, the first death occurred in the camp. We had to decide upon a burial ground at once, since the climate allowed of no delay in such matters.

Colonel Williamson and I took a walk around the precincts of our camp and came upon a small clearing by the river about 20yds square, surrounded by tall clumps of bamboo and trees and with a blue jacaranda bush flowering vividly at one side. It seemed a perfect site.

There had once been a native hut there, but no trace of it remained except the small open space where it had once stood. The grave was dug, the interment took place with all reverence and a wooden cross was put up with the man's name, regimental number and regiment carved on it. That was the beginning of a cemetery which ultimately contained over fifteen hundred graves of British, Australian and Dutch soldiers, sailors and airmen.

Foreseeing that we must perforce expect other deaths, we marked out a large rectangular patch about half an acre in extent, and volunteers were quickly forthcoming to clear and level the area. Even before this was done, there were several more graves, and week by week the number increased. As time went on, flowerbeds were dug, an archway of timber built at the entrance and a border gay with flowers grown from seeds gathered from native gardens was planted round all four sides. Very soon our small cemetery became a sanctuary of peace and beauty visited by many. It was always the haven of vividly coloured butterflies and birds of many kinds which added to the beauty of the flowers.

Time went on, Colonel Williamson had been moved upriver to another camp and I was in command at Chungkai. Our half acre was almost filled, with about a hundred graves, and it became necessary either to enlarge the area or select another. I took one or two friends with me to prospect, and we decided that though it was not practicable to enlarge further there were possibilities of clearing a space in the jungle on a larger piece of level ground separated from the existing cemetery by a small gulley.

Here there was unlimited space if it was cleared, and a start was made forthwith. All the trees were cut down except one magnificent specimen which we left standing almost in the centre, bamboos, undergrowth and tree roots were laboriously dug and hauled out by gangs of officers and men and the debris burned on site. Then the ground was levelled, and before long we had a clearing twice as large as the original one.

By this time, we had persuaded the Japs to let us have a staff of grave diggers and gardeners for the purpose. Most of them were older or more senior officers and men whom we wished to protect from the rigorous hardship of work on the railway, and as they continued the work of clearing, so they also set about the happier task of levelling and beautifying the whole area. Grass was encouraged to grow and was trimmed with improvised implements and kept at about six inches high.

The graves were planned in symmetrical rows with three wide aisles running lengthways, eight graves between each aisle. At the entrance, borders were dug and filled with plants moved from the first cemetery and many kinds of gaily coloured flowers grown from seeds collected locally. Down each side ran a scarlet-flowered hibiscus hedge struck from cuttings, with a wide border in front of it filled with flowers, predominant among them being huge clumps of canna lilies, a blaze of reds and yellows.

At first, rough crosses made of any kind of wood available were set up at the head of each grave, but white ants soon ate them away at ground level and the number of graves grew with such rapidity that it was impossible to keep pace with them. However, a plan was made and kept in our Camp Office with a complete record of each man's name, rank, regimental number and regiment, as well as the date and cause of his death and his religious denomination. This record was eventually brought home and handed over to the War Graves Commission.

From time to time we asked the Japanese for wood with which to make crosses, but it was not until 1944 that they eventually supplied a sufficient quantity of suitable sawn hardwood. A party of Australians then volunteered to make crosses and carve the particulars on them. They made a superb job of it, and eventually every grave had a neat wooden cross with rank, name, number, regiment and denomination carved on it, the lettering being painted black.

After the officers were separated from the other ranks, the men maintained the beauty of the cemetery until Chungkai was abandoned in the early summer of 1945.

Chapter 22

Mass Hysteria

Probably this account of two very strange happenings would fit better amongst the stories of medical cases, but here they are and they were two of the strangest occurrences of my whole time as a prisoner of war. The first incident happened at Ban Pong in the horrible camp which we were put in when we first arrived in Siam. One night, 'lights out' had sounded and the camp lay in darkness and silence. The long huts, each holding about 100 men, lay parallel to each other and about two yards apart. In the officers' hut, most of us were asleep or lying quietly on our hard bamboo beds, when suddenly there were shouts from a man in the next hut; then silence for two or three seconds, followed by a crescendo of shouting until there was complete bedlam and sounds of people crashing about in the darkness and making for the doorways at the hut ends to escape.

Several of us leapt out of bed, slipping on boots and grabbing our electric torches, which up to that time the Japs had not taken from us, and dashed into the next hut from which the noise was coming. A few loud and terse orders obtained silence, and then we asked what it was all about.

One man appeared to have been certain that some large animal had walked over his feet; his shouts had communicated his fear to those on each side of him, and in a matter of seconds the nameless terror had spread like wildfire through the whole hut. We shone our torches all round the hut and under the beds and assured the men that it was all pure imagination; but even then they were only partly reassured. However, as quiet once more prevailed, we returned to our beds – but not for long!

Within a few minutes the whole thing was repeated, and once again we had to crash in and walk up and down the hut shining our torches into every corner and talking to the men, until taut nerves had relaxed and fear had dissipated.

The second occasion was about two years later at Chungkai, at a time when nerves were at a point of considerable tension. One bright moonlit night just after dark, we were having a concert, and about two thousand men were sitting together on an open piece of ground which we normally used for games. I was pretty well at the back of the crowd sitting on the ground with Major Innes, when suddenly there were shouts on our left and men began jumping to their feet. In a moment there was pandemonium, and the mass of men started to run in terror away from the point where the shouts had started.

Innes and I jumped to our feet and stood yelling at the men to stop them, but with a few exceptions they took not the slightest notice, though a number of others were also trying to stem the stampede. In a few seconds the area was clear except for the few who stood fast wondering what it was all about.

In front of the stage were a number of stretcher cases brought from the hospital by the medical orderlies to listen to the concert. The orderlies stood their ground manfully and laid about them right and left in their efforts to protect their charges from the milling mass of men fleeing over and past them. Hundreds dived panic-stricken under the side walls of the hospital that ran alongside the open space, then clambered over the luckless bedridden patients inside, continuing their aimless flight from the unknown danger until physical exhaustion or the quiet of their surroundings eventually pulled them up and brought them to the realization that they were not being pursued.

While all this was happening, I thought of all sorts of possibilities, such as a Japanese or Korean gone berserk, a maddened water buffalo running amok or some other fierce animal invading the camp, but there was nothing to see at all; just a bare expanse of ground where shortly before there had been two thousand happy, laughing men.

The concert ended abruptly, with the entertainers still standing on the stage facing a deserted auditorium and all of us wondering what it was all about. Eventually, the explanation was forthcoming. One man sitting at the outside of the crowd had spotted a small snake about a foot long in close proximity to some part of his anatomy and with some justification had jumped to his feet with a shout of warning to his companions. From that small incident, complete panic had started.

It was entirely due to overwrought nerves and undernourished bodies.

Chapter 23

Attack from the Air

Towards the latter part of 1944, air activity by the Allied forces increased considerably, and it became an almost daily occurrence to hear a recce plane droning over us far up in the stratosphere, usually too high to be visible. Similarly, flights of Liberators began to pay attention to the railway, bombing it at various points where there were bridges or viaducts.

One of the most vulnerable points was at Tamarkan, about three miles from Chungkai, where the Japanese had first built a wooden bridge over the Quaiyai river and had then substituted a steel one, which they had dismantled in Java and had brought to Siam. Both bridges had of course been erected with PoW labour. Several attacks had been made on the wooden one with some measure of success, and as soon as the steel one was complete it was similarly attacked.

One day, my eye was suddenly caught by a glint of silver in the sky far to the north, and in a few moments I could see it was a flight of Liberators approaching over the hills and gleaming in the brilliant sunshine. They came in high over the bridge and circled round several times, whereupon most of our Korean guards dived for their air-raid shelters and remained there.

One after the other the great planes zoomed down over the bridge, and we watched as stick after stick of bombs went hurtling down around the target, sending up clouds of debris and dust. For a time the Japanese battery of AA guns went into action, but without effect, and in a short time they ceased firing, no doubt having received a fair share of the bombs. It was an inspiring sight for us and was over all too soon; having done their job, the planes flew off home apparently none the worse for the AA fire. The steel bridge was damaged and put out of action for the time being, but it was not until a later date that it was finally destroyed.

The most spectacular raid of all happened some months later, when another flight of Liberators came over just before dusk and attacked the Japanese headquarters at Kanburi.

On this occasion, about a dozen planes appeared and circled round and round, pinpointing their target on a course which brought them almost over our heads time after time. Stick after stick of bombs was dropped with deadly accuracy on the area occupied by the Japs, in which they had a considerable supply depot and a small-arms ammunition dump. The raid went on for about half an hour.

Some time previously, Kokobo had made us dig slit trenches round our huts and had ordered us to occupy them whenever there was an air raid warning. We in Camp Headquarters had no desire to have to stay in a trench on these occasions, and after much argument had succeeded in persuading the Japs to allow me and one or two of my staff to walk about if we wished to – officially in order to see that everybody else was in their trenches, but actually in order that we might see what was going on.

When this raid started and looked like being a spectacular affair, I decided that the river bank would be the best vantage point. The cookhouses were all near the river, so on the pretext of going to see that the cooks were taking cover, I made my way there and had a magnificent view of the bombing going on about a mile and a half away. Meanwhile, Kokobo and his men had descended into their foxholes and dugouts, Kokobo with his customary supply of local brandy!

The bombing started a fire in the small-arms dump which added to the turmoil, and volleys of 'ammo' continued to explode long after the planes had gone home. As soon as the last plane had departed, I made my way back towards my Headquarters in the darkness which had now fallen, and just before I reached it I heard the sound of a party approaching at the double. As the party came towards me, I saw it was Kokobo leading a troop of tin-hatted Koreans with his great sword carried at the 'ready', so I stepped to one side and stopped.

So did he, and then he came up to me yelling a torrent of Japanese, waving his sword and flashing it round my head. For a few moments, I must admit, my heart was in my mouth. He was obviously fairly drunk and I couldn't understand a word of what he was saying, never having made any attempt to learn more than the essential few words of Japanese which we all learnt. I decided that my best hope of salvation was to stand still and hope he was not too drunk to control his actions, while I shouted for an interpreter.

In a few moments, a Dutch interpreter arrived upon whom Kokobo turned and repeated the display. The Dutchman then turned to me and said, 'Kokobo says that parachutists have landed and he is going to kill them. If you allow anyone to leave the camp while he is away, he will cut off your head.'

I assured him that I would take every precaution to prevent such a thing happening, whereupon he barked an order to his men and they disappeared into the night to fight the non-existent parachutists!

Chapter 24

The Camp Police

As I have already mentioned, we had our own force of military police in the camp at Chungkai. They were originally formed in the early days when we first arrived and it became necessary to safeguard the property of men who were out working for the Japs from the thefts which regrettably became all too frequent as the standard of morale fell among a limited number of men for whom the future appeared to depend upon the survival of the fittest, and thus on the ability to buy extra food. The meagre pay of ten and fifteen cents a day for those who could work, and nothing for those who were too sick to, could only lead to temptation, which some were unable to resist.

When I took over the camp, I re-organized the police under Captain Robin Calderwood who had joined the Malayan Volunteers and had been an officer in the Malayan Police in peacetime. He selected Lieutenant Peck of the Beds and Herts as his APM. Peck had been a constable in the Metropolitan Police before the war and was a quiet, capable and efficient officer.

These two went through the existing force of a dozen or so men with a toothcomb, returning one or two to ordinary duties and then adding to the numbers of the force by careful selection, until they had about twenty men of the highest moral and physical standard, led by a splendid warrant officer in RSM Low of the Gordons.

The force had its own quarters in a corner of the camp and they kept it in a state of spotless cleanliness which, together with their smart turnout and military bearing, was at all times a model and inspiration to the rest of the camp. Their duties were at that stage confined to the limits of the camp, where they patrolled day and night, preventing theft and subsequent black-market dealings with Thais and in many cases arresting the perpetrators of these undesirable practices in the act.

The camp was some fifty acres in extent at this time, with nothing more than a light bamboo fence surrounding it which presented no difficulties to anyone desirous of going out into the surrounding jungle to trade with the local inhabitants. In fact, the fence was more a token boundary than anything else. We had no desire to prevent anyone from going out on any legitimate expedition whatsoever, and there were many men who did so for the simple pleasure of escaping for an hour or two from the confines of the camp. Some decided that money with which to buy eggs, fruit and suchlike aids to the maintenance of health was more important than the possession of signet rings, fountain pens for which they had no use and watches which they might lose or break at any time. Any of these possessions would fetch varying sums up to fifty or even a hundred Thai *ticals* or dollars, and for a dollar one could buy twenty duck eggs in those days, though as time went on the price doubled and trebled.

Tobacco and cigarettes were in short supply, too, and a number of more enterprising and commercially minded individuals went into business with the Chinese and Thais, making clandestine sorties into the surrounding jungle, where they bought large quantities of native-grown tobacco, which they brought back, converted into cigarettes and sold at a highly remunerative price in the camp.

The Dutch were the main instigators of this trade and they built up a number of flourishing concerns, employing numbers of their semi-sick brethren in the manufacture of cigarettes under proprietary brands such as 'Blue Cross', 'Big Tree' and suchlike names. The British were not long in following their example, and in course of time the tobacco trade assumed a turnover of many hundreds of dollars a week; so big, in fact, that at a later date when we were in great need of all the money we could obtain in order to buy eggs, fruit, sugar and even quinine – the latter in secret from the Thais at exorbitant prices – we hit upon the plan of imposing a revenue tax on the 'tobacco barons' which brought in the surprisingly large sum of some 800 dollars per month for the benefit of the men in the Camp Hospital. Some of the tobacco barons were reputed to be worth hundreds if not thousands of dollars and could well afford this levy on their profits!

Unfortunately, there were other occupants of the camp whose activities were not so blameless. These were the people who derived a remunerative return outside the confines of the camp from the sale of stolen goods. Blankets and clothing of any kind fetched a good price from the Thais, as did fountain pens, rings and other treasured possessions. Even though our police were successful in many instances in frustrating these attempts before they matured, they could have been far more efficacious had they been able to work outside the camp instead of only inside.

Whenever the police caught anyone, he was brought up before his battalion commander and punished in accordance with a scale which we worked out and which took the form of periods of extra fatigues about the camp under the supervision of his own battalion, or in more serious cases, varying periods of detention in the camp police barracks, in which case the prisoner was subjected to strict discipline and the daily performance of any menial and uncongenial tasks which required doing about the camp.

The Japanese acknowledged this system without question and seemed to approve of our efforts to maintain discipline. Unfortunately, there were occasions when the Japs caught our fellows selling to the Thais or buying tobacco in the native *kampongs*, and then they insisted on dealing with them themselves. When Kokobo was in command of the camp, he invariably sent for me to be present while he meted out punishment, and there were frequent occasions when I had to stand by and watch him administer severe face-slappings. The Japanese interpreter would question the men and report to Kokobo, who then decided the severity of the face-slapping called for.

Kokobo was only about five feet tall, so he used to stand on a platform in front of the culprits with a bucket of water beside him into which he dipped his hand; he would then go down the line administering terrific slaps on both cheeks, the object of wetting his hands being to make the blows sting more! Invariably, at first, he took no notice of my protestations, probably because he couldn't understand English and because he had not gained the respect for me which I am glad to say he did acquire as time went on. At the end of these performances we were all summarily dismissed, the victims to stagger away rubbing their stinging faces and me boiling with futile wrath and indignation. However, he came to realize in the course of time that I was trying to maintain discipline too and gradually began to ask my opinion about the punishment he proposed to administer.

In cases of face-slapping, my opinion didn't really amount to much, because it was purely a matter of whether the luckless victim got a severe bashing or a less severe one; but where it did help was after he had devised a form of solitary confinement in some revolting little cells which he had had constructed. They were about five feet square and made of solid bamboo, with no window and a mud floor. In fairness to him, he was in the habit of confining his own men in them with impartiality on numerous occasions. Most of the Koreans could speak a few words of English by this time and they christened this primitive gaol the 'No Good House', by which name it came to be universally known.

It was usually reserved for the perpetrators of more serious offences when caught by the Japanese, and Kokobo's sentences might consist of any period up to thirty days. Having decided that the case was proved, he would tell his interpreter to ask me how many days I thought the sentence should be. Knowing that it was a matter of bargaining for the lowest figure possible and not for an acquittal, I used to start as low down the scale as possible, and we invariably effected a compromise somewhere in between.

At first, he had Korean guards on duty outside day and night, but after a time he allowed our police to take over some of the duty; this was an advance on the earlier regulations as it made it possible for us to smuggle in a little more on occasions than the plain rice and water diet which was all he would allow. At night, Korean armed sentries were on duty, but as they had equal cause to hate the No Good House, most of them had a sneaking sympathy with the PoW inmates and would quite often connive at our attempts to ameliorate the plight of the victims.

It sounds remarkable, but it is a fact that after a spell of even as long as thirty days the victims used to come out weighing more than when they went in and, so far as could be ascertained, in no lower physical state, although naturally looking paler than the rest of us who lived in perpetual sunshine.

One day, Kokobo complained that our camp police were not preventing men from going out into the jungle and selling things to the Thais. This was the opportunity we had been waiting for. We had been finding it increasingly difficult to obtain batteries and spare parts for our secret wireless set, and it was most desirable that we should have more contact with the Thais for this and many other reasons; so I seized the chance of telling him that if he would allow us to increase the police force and would give them passes to work outside the camp as well as inside, they would undoubtedly be more effective.

In this we were at one with the Japanese, since we were equally anxious to prevent the sale of stolen property. Kokobo fell for the suggestion and we doubled the police force and won a most valuable concession. From then onwards they had a great deal more freedom, which they put to excellent use, but not always in the manner intended by Kokobo! They were able to patrol the local *kampongs* and succeeded in apprehending quite a number of our illicit traffickers, bringing them back by devious paths into the camp, where they were duly tried and punished by their respective battalion officers, all unknown to the Japanese.

The only snag was that the Japanese could not understand why we never appeared to catch anyone outside the camp, but we managed to get round that by saying that the police were being so efficient that they had put a stop to the traffic.

Thereafter, on many occasions, members of the police would walk serenely past the Japanese guardhouse with their pockets full of electric torch batteries for the wireless set, or with packets of the invaluable Emetine for the treatment of amoebic dysentery cases, purchased at exorbitant prices from the Thais, who were able to obtain it in Bangkok and sell it to us, the purchase money being provided from the secret camp funds.

When we first came up to Siam, General Percival issued an order that all battalion commanders would continue to publish battalion orders at intervals to the effect that we were still on active service. The purpose of this was to enable commanding officers to maintain discipline and if necessary to convene field general courts martial. In Chungkai, as in other camps up and down the railway, such action was necessary from time to time, and here again our corps of military police performed a most useful duty in the courts and in carrying out the sentences when necessary.

During the time I was in charge of Chungkai, I had to convene several FGCMs. We had copies of King's Regulations and the Manual of Military Law, and there were several officers formerly in the JAG [Judge Advocate General] Department. It was therefore practicable to hold such courts in our own lines in accordance with the prescribed regulations, although obviously certain details of procedure had to be adapted to our unique surroundings and conditions. Sentences were pronounced and carried out with justice and in good faith, but of course all records were destroyed before our release, though that intention was not divulged at the time or such measures would have had no value.

On one occasion when a FGCM was being held in one of the huts in the camp, and when we were most anxious that the reason for it should not be known by the Japanese, who might have decided to deal with the case them-selves, Kokobo took it into his head to have a walk round the camp and in due course came to the hut where the court was sitting. A kind of electric shock ran through the assembled court at his unexpected appearance at the entrance. As it happened, he had no interpreter with him, but he knew a few words of English and, turning to the nearest officer, pointed at the members of the court and said, 'What is it?'

With a dry mouth the officer replied, 'Court martial'.

'Quartermaster?' repeated Kokobo. 'Okay,' and walked out!

I think it is true to say that no other camp had at any time such a highly organized and efficient police force, and by their example, bearing and behaviour these men contributed immensely to the high standard of morale which the camp eventually attained. At a later date, however, their activi-ties were severely curtailed by the Japanese, and finally they were disbanded when the officers were separated from the men and removed to Kanburi in the spring of 1945.

Chapter 25

The Exodus from Chungkai

As 1944 drew to its close, the Japs began to talk of moving all officers to a camp by themselves. At first it was just an unwelcome rumour, but gradually it became obvious that this was their intention. They began to tighten up a lot on our freedom – what little we had – and ordered us to hand in rings, watches, fountain pens, cigarette cases and anything else which was saleable. They also declared it an offence for anyone to have notebooks or writing materials in his possession. Several searches of the huts were made and a lot of our personal possessions were confiscated. Fortunately, I had buried my diary and various other incriminating papers long before.

The area of the camp was reduced and a fence constructed across the middle which excluded the church and my headquarters, though they told us to make plans for a new headquarters in a different spot within the circumscribed area; this was done and the building more or less completed before they started to erect the fence.

We were told about the proposed move in January and were ordered to plan things in such a way that all the key positions in the camp could be handed over to warrant officers and senior NCOs at short notice. Accordingly, a hand-picked team was earmarked for the jobs, and I appointed RSM Edwards of the Staffordshire Regiment as the future Camp Commandant and began to show him all I could of the kind of work he would have to do. The same procedure was followed with the other posts in our administration. After we left, these WOs and NCOs did a very fine job until the day of our eventual release.

The order to move came one day in February, and there was a fevered period in the next twenty-four hours or so, packing up and handing over so that the organization of the camp might continue without too much of an upset. A few weeks before this actually happened, the two Webber brothers came to see me and said that they wanted to take their wireless set with them. We knew that all our kit would be searched very thoroughly before we left Chungkai, as indeed it was, and we were told by officers already at Kanburi that we should be searched again when we arrived there and that the standard of thoroughness was pretty high. This also proved to be the case.

I advised the Webbers most strongly not to tempt providence, pointing out that they had had a remarkably successful run of luck so far and had better leave it at that. However, they were desperately keen to take it and begged me to give them permission, saying they had evolved a really safe plan. Eventually I agreed, though with considerable misgivings.

First of all, they sent the electric torch batteries in small lots entrusted to various people who used to come and go between Chungkai and Tamarkan camps on errands connected with PoW records, trips to attend the dentist, etc. Tamarkan camp was in the process of being evacuated after frequent bombing raids by American Liberators had been made on the railway bridge close beside it, several of which had unfortunately hit the PoW camp and caused a number of casualties. The Japanese were not unduly concerned that we had suffered casualties, but they didn't enjoy being bombed themselves and decided to move. There were still a number of British there, but the huts which had been evacuated were being pulled down and the bamboo poles were being taken to Kanburi to enlarge the camp for the influx of officers from all the other camps.

The torch batteries were handed over to trusted friends, and when the working parties of officers from Kanburi came up for their next load of bamboo poles, the batteries were pushed down the hollow poles, plugged in with mud and carried back to Kanburi, where they were duly retrieved and hidden away. I don't know exactly who made all these elaborate arrangements, but at any rate that part of the transfer was accomplished safely.

On the morning of our departure we spent hours out on the large parade ground at Chungkai with all our baggage laid out in the blazing hot sun, while inquisitive and aggressive Japanese members of the *Kempeitai*, assisted by a number of rather bored Korean guards, meticulously searched all our stuff. I remember having a horribly tense feeling while all this was going on as I did not know what plan had been evolved for taking the wireless set and I had a nasty feeling that at any moment there would be a shout of fury and excitement from one of the *Kempeitai* as he discovered the set in somebody's belongings. The Webbers had said that they thought it better that no one at the time should know where it was, since it was well known that the *Kempeitai* would stop at nothing to extract information from anyone who they thought had any knowledge which would be valuable to them. However, nothing of any moment was discovered, and after several hours in the baking sun, during which we were not allowed to leave the square, we were ordered to embark on a fleet of barges for the short trip downstream to Kanburi, about five barges being towed by an antique motor barge, or pompom, driven by coconut oil.

In some ways we were quite sorry to be leaving Chungkai. Unpleasant though much of our time there had been, we had made the best of it, and we felt that the future was likely to be more unpleasant, while there was no river and no freedom of movement in the much smaller Kanburi camp, which was already known to many of us. As we drifted away down the river, the troops left on shore stood waving and shouting 'Au revoir' to us until the camp was lost to sight round a bend. On the way down we met a barge coming upriver with our old Camp Commander Kokobo, who also gave us a cheerful grin and a wave as he passed. That was the last I saw of him.

During the search on the parade ground, one thing that had rather surprised me was the sight of the camp's Provost Marshal, Captain Robin Calderwood, lying on a bamboo stretcher. He had been quite fit the day before, but when I enquired about his trouble he told me he had had a nasty fall and hurt his back. He was carried down to the barges and put on board with great care by some of his friends; at the other end they carried him to the new camp, and he lay on his stretcher while another thorough search of all our kit was carried out by the camp guards, after which he was borne off to the hospital hut.

On arrival there, his back became suddenly better, the bamboo stretcher was quickly dismantled and various parts of our wireless set were removed from its hollow poles. Furthermore, little did the Japs know that the small wooden stool which Max Webber carried with him sported a false bottom, in which the rest of the set was concealed! And so, thanks to the intrepid daring of these young men, we arrived in our new home still able to hear what was happening in the outside world.

Kanburi was well known to many of us from previous trips there on one pretext or another: to buy stores for the canteen, to visit the dentist at one of the other camps (this was always a good line when we had no dentist in our own camp), or having been put on some working party required for a job of loading or unloading rations there. The Siamese there were always friendly and sympathetic towards us since they too loathed the Japs and had suffered severely at their hands on many occasions.

The new camp, at least new to us, was about half a mile from the town across a flat open space which had formerly been used as an emergency landing ground, and our way led through the old fortress with its high walls of mud and stone dating back to the seventeenth century. On arrival we sensed at once a more hostile atmosphere than at Chungkai, and we had already been warned that Captain Noguchi, the Commandant, and his staff were a thoroughly bad lot, so first impressions were distinctly depressing. As already stated, our kit was once more searched in no uncertain manner and a few more things were confiscated, though by this time few people had anything of value left. Various parties of officers had already arrived from other camps; they gave us a warm welcome, and we were all glad to meet many old friends we had not seen for months or even years. They welcomed us to 'the fold', helped to carry our possessions to the huts and showed us the essential features of our new 'home'.

The total area of the camp was about 12 acres, but the eighty or so Japs and Koreans occupied eight acres and allowed us a space of four acres for about 3,000 officers, so that being shown round was quite a short process! As may be imagined, we were fairly thick on the ground; in fact, by the time everyone had arrived it was never possible to be more than about six feet from your next door neighbour at any time. The living space allocated to each of us was an area of very hard and knobbly bamboo bench 7ft long by 2ft 6ins wide, and on this and above it on the bamboo walls were draped ourselves and all our worldly possessions. Tidiness was therefore essential.

The camp was administered much more strictly by the Japs than Chungkai had been, and we had to salute all Japanese officers and NCOs at any distance. Failure to do so meant a 'bashing'. Colonel Toosey, the CO of 135 Field Regiment, was the British Camp Commandant and he had an unenviable task which he performed with great ability. Before coming here, he had been Commandant at a camp near Ban Pong called Nom Pladuk, which had been badly bombed by accident during a raid by the Allies in which they dropped a stick of bombs on the camp, which was close to a railway marshalling yard, and killed about 90 of our men. When this camp was evacuated in consequence, he went to Tamarkan, where the same thing happened, though fortunately with fewer casualties. At Chungkai we were fortunate in being well away from any potential targets and used to watch the raids in safety, for which we were devoutly thankful.

Having no responsibilities in Kanburi camp, I was quite glad of a rest for the time being, particularly as I had had a rather troublesome small tropical ulcer on my ankle. I was now able to rest it for the first time, and this soon caused an improvement.

We gradually sorted ourselves out as time went on and found occupations of one sort and another suited to our varying states of health and vigour. The older and more senior officers became vegetable peelers, and the number of little onions like shallots I peeled in the first few weeks was just legion. This became too sedentary an occupation after a time, and I joined the Peanut Bashers brigade; quite a pleasant occupation calling for considerably more energy and having the added advantage that when one had 'bashed' the peanuts into butter, one was entitled to scrape off what remained sticking to the basher and eat it! Since peanut butter has a fairly high vitamin content, this had considerable value, quite apart from the pleasure of tasting something other than rice.

In making the butter we adopted the native method which consisted of a mortar made of a teak log hollowed out and a pestle of similar wood looking rather like a large sized Indian club and about three times as heavy. It was quite hard work, particularly in our unfit condition. The proceeds of our industry were delivered to the canteen and sold daily over the counter in five-cent pats. There were three processes in reducing the nuts to butter: first they were reduced to a rough squashy mass, after which one handed them on to the second squad, who reduced them by similar means to a finer form of porridge, stopping when there were no lumps left and when the oil in the nuts caused the mass to look like putty. The final process of refinement to the finished article was done on tables made of the ubiquitous fish-box lids, on which the mass was rolled out still finer with the aid of glass bottles used as rolling pins.

All work in this camp was done by the officers, there being only a handful of other ranks who were used by the Japanese to do chores for them and as boot repairers and tailors.

We had a large cookhouse with rows of bamboo fires burning under *qualis* set in mud. Using earth removed in various excavations, some enterprising people started our own brickworks, with the products of which, in due course, many things were built, among them being a really magnificent bakery, the ovens being constructed from 40 gallon diesel oil drums which the Japs were persuaded to part with. This was not entirely a new idea, as we had already done the same thing at Chungkai with considerable success, and in these ovens our cooks were able to produce some very welcome bread, even though it was made of rice flour.

Another industry which called for considerable inventive genius was the paper factory, which in the course of time produced a welcome if limited supply of paper for one specific but universal purpose, made from banana leaves and one or two other ingredients of which I am uncertain, though I think one was lime.

Our water supply came from two wells in the camp; one, mainly used for washing, was within a few yards of the ablution benches and latrines, though the filtering powers of the alluvial sand and clay soil must have been fairly effective as the water seemed quite pure; the other well, rather further from the latrines, was used for all cooking purposes.

The canteen which had been in operation before we were transferred to the camp was quite an efficient business organization though not quite so large or comprehensive in its trade as the one at Chungkai, for the reason that Noguchi and his men were much less co-operative than Chungkai's Japanese staff.

When we first arrived, we merely occupied any huts without reference to seniority, but rather according to regimental or other friendships. After a while the Japanese decided to reorganize us to some extent and ordained that all officers of field rank should move into the hut nearest to their own part of the camp. This having been done, the other officers somewhat unkindly christened our hut 'The Imperial War Museum'!

The only spaces for recreation were the parade ground, which was just big enough to hold us drawn up in mass formation, between the huts and the canteen, and a broad road at the opposite end of the long huts running the full length of the camp. This road was about 150yds long and about 20yds wide, and many of us must have walked several hundred miles up and down it in search of daily exercise during the ensuing months.

When we first arrived, there was already a fairly wide and deep moat all round the camp with a high barbed wire fence along the outer bank and machine gun posts at intervals all round. However, the Japs evidently intended to take no chances with us and made us dig the moat still deeper; the resulting soil was formed into a high bank on the outer side and then surmounted by the barbed wire fence and machine gun posts as before. They then went one better still and made us build a bamboo stockade as well, so that we could not see out.

After the wide expanse and comparative 'freedom' of our previous camp, we 'Old Chungkaians' found our extremely restricted space pretty irksome and the close proximity of one's fellow beings on all occasions difficult to get used to. I think it is to our credit that I can never remember anyone giving vent to his feelings, in spite of the physical and mental strain of living cheek by jowl with the same people day and night for months on end.

After a month or so of more or less enforced idleness, in which my ankle had improved a great deal, I began to want something more energetic to do and volunteered with Major Innes to join a party which went out under escort about three times a week to Tamarkan camp about three miles away to continue the work of dismantling the old huts there and to bring back long bamboo poles which were required for building new huts in our own camp.

The way to Tamarkan led through the outskirts of Kanburi village, past a large Buddhist temple, upon the steps of which we often sat for a rest on the return journey, and along a sandy track through the jungle with now and then a native *kampong* or a single Siamese hut. At many of these, the occupants were willing enough to sell us bananas and cakes of various kinds, and so long as our Korean guards were fairly certain that no Japanese were in the vicinity, they would usually let us buy from the Siamese. It was a real treat to get out into the fresh air and greenery of the jungle, with all its birds and butterflies and vivid colours, and we really enjoyed these excursions in spite of the fact that we were only doing the work of native coolies!

On arrival at Tamarkan we usually managed to persuade the Jap guards to let us bathe in the river, which was a real joy and absolute bliss after weeks of washing in a bucket of tepid and rather stale water in the camp. The river here was quite shallow and beautifully clear and warm with a lovely pebbly bed, and one could lie in it and wallow for half an hour and forget for a while the unpleasantness to which we shortly had to return. Another pleasant feature of the neighbourhood of Tamarkan was a grove of mango trees bearing enormous quantities of fruit, which we gathered and brought back in haver-sacks while the season lasted.

There was always the added excitement that an American force of Liberators might suddenly appear at any moment, bent on the further destruction of the railway bridge; in that case we should have been in a very vulnerable position, but though we saw them flying over for other and more distant targets on several occasions, they never coincided with our visits. One evening, however, after we had been there during the morning, they did attack the bridge and completely destroyed it, to our great delight. We had a grandstand view from the camp and watched the sticks of bombs falling while the local Japanese battery of ack-ack guns blazed away at the planes with no visible results whatsoever.

Our job on these trips was to collect two long bamboo poles to each pair of officers and carry them back to Kanburi on our shoulders; if they were very big ones, we took only one and carried an end each. In our reduced state, they were quite a heavy load, being usually about 30ft long and about 4ins thick at the butt; at first they made our shoulders rather sore, but we got quite used to the work after a few trips. We always had a halt about halfway back and bought more bananas and cakes whenever the coast was clear of Japanese. Eventually, the Japs decided that we had brought enough material for what was required, and we were very disappointed when our excursions came to an end and there was no way of getting away from this depressing and overcrowded place for a breath of clean air unpolluted by the constant smell of latrines.

The air raid on Tamarkan bridge was one of the most enjoyable days we spent during the last summer of our captivity – even though in its later stages the raid developed in a less pleasant manner and became too personal altogether for our comfort. It happened one day in June. We became con-scious of the familiar drone of approaching Liberators from the direction of Burma which had recently become a regular occurrence and one which always filled us with feelings of excitement and joy, especially when they came over near enough for us to feel that the occupants could see us down below. Our places were not marked as PoW camps in any way, but we felt sure by this time that the airmen knew where all our camps lay, so as a rule we had little fear of being bombed, although there was always a slight feeling of relief if they didn't fly directly over us as we could never be quite certain on this point!

On this occasion, about a dozen appeared in the sky to the north–west and after circling round high up, began to drop down to about 2,000ft. One after another, they flew in over the railway bridge on their bombing line. As soon as the Japs heard them coming they rushed out blowing bugles and yelling at the top of their voices, ordering us to get into the shallow and quite inadequate trenches outside our huts, then disappearing into their own much deeper and better constructed funk-holes.

From where I was, I could see the Liberators flying round and round, taking no notice of the spasmodic firing of the one and only Jap AA battery near the bridge and dropping their sticks of bombs, from which rose clouds of smoke and debris flung hundreds of feet in the air. Round and round they went, apparently untouched by the AA fire, until eventually they silenced the battery. Previous raids had damaged the bridge without putting it completely out of use, but on this occasion they really meant business and succeeded, as we were able to see on our next bamboo-carrying expedition.

Meanwhile, we squatted in our trenches enjoying the sight, but a few minutes later, we were glad even of their slight protection. Two of the Liberators spotted an engine in a siding just outside the camp and came to investigate. One of them approached it on a line which brought him straight over the camp after passing over the target. As he came in on his run, we saw bombs falling out from under the plane in quick succession. For a moment I thought they were all coming straight for me and watched them with a kind of mesmerized fascination. Then they began to straighten out and it seemed as if they would fall short of the camp all right but, mistiming his release, the bomb-aimer had let four of them go too late and they actually fell inside the camp just behind the canteen, about 50yds in front of me.

I watched them falling until they reached the level of the canteen roof and then I ducked to the bottom of the shallow trench, which Captain Freddie Hibbert and I were sharing. There was a tremendous roar, the ground shook and earth began to fall on us, but that was all as far as we were concerned. Unfortunately, there were several people in the canteen, mostly Dutch officers, of whom three were killed and two slightly wounded.

This was not the end of the excitement. One of the Korean guards, a little braver than the rest, opened up on the plane with his Lewis gun. It appeared to do no harm to the plane, but evidently annoyed the Americans inside, who thereupon flew low round the camp several times, spraying it with their .50in machine guns. This wasn't nearly so amusing for us as watching them bomb the bridge. Tracer bullets zipped through the camp in all directions, and Freddie and I pressed ourselves to the bottom of our little trench. Suddenly a bright flash passed in front of my nose; Freddie lay quite still and I thought he had been killed, but he hadn't been touched.

When the firing stopped and the plane flew off, we raised our heads and about a foot from where they had been was a neat hole in the side of the trench where the tracer bullet had struck. A few yards away, another shirt-less officer was examining with interest a red weal across his stomach. When the firing started, he had been caught some distance from a trench and had dropped into a shallow ditch beside the road through the camp. After a time, feeling cramped in one position, he raised himself on his elbows to turn over at the precise moment that the bullet arrived. Had he not done so, it would have gone straight through him!

After that experience, we were inclined to view the close approach of our American friends in the air with certain misgivings. Occasionally a solitary plane would come over very high, and for some time after it had disappeared we would see what looked like a football floating miles up in the air. Gradually the football would grow bigger and more diffuse and become thousands of leaflets floating down slowly in the clear atmosphere. It was fascinating to watch them gradually getting nearer and spreading out, drifting in the light currents of air and usually taking at least a couple of hours to reach the ground.

Of course, we always hoped that some of them would fall in the camp, and once or twice they did. On these occasions the Japs rushed about for-bidding us to pick them up and threatening dire punishments to anyone seen doing so, but of course we succeeded in spite of their threats. Usually they were written in Siamese or Chinese but that presented no difficulties as we had linguists in every tongue among our numbers. One lot were written in English and told us to keep smiling, ending up with 'It's in the Bag!' That message cheered us a lot.

By the end of May one really serious difficulty had arisen: our wireless bat-teries had run out in spite of the most limited use of the set, and supervision was so close that there was no possibility of replacing them. Consequently, we had to rely on any scraps of outside information we could glean and try and piece them together in the hope that out of them we could obtain some idea of the trend of events in the outside world. An Intelligence Centre was formed consisting of a selected group of officers, most of whom had had some previous experience of this kind of work, and from the meagre scraps of information brought in to them day by day they managed to extract a surprising amount of interesting, cheering and, as was subsequently proved, accurate information.

Deprived of any form of exercise other than the necessary camp duties and chores, some of the younger officers rigged up a basketball pitch and formed an Inter-hut League which was a source of much excitement for players and supporters. We also organized physical training squads of varying degrees of severity according to the age and condition of those taking part, all of which activities helped to maintain our strength and to pass the time.

At some previous period there had been a theatre of sorts constructed opposite the parade ground, but it had been out of use for many months. This was now renewed and an orchestra was formed, chiefly from the former members of our Chungkai orchestra and augmented by various musicians who had come from other camps. Unfortunately, Noguchi and his staff were less tolerant than the Chungkai Japanese and severely limited the time for practice and performances; but we were usually allowed one show per week, which gave great pleasure to both performers and audience alike.

The hospital consisted of one hut at the farthest end of the camp from the Japanese, and here were a number of serious and pathetic cases, as well as many of slighter degree. The most serious was a young American airman who had developed a tumour on the brain and lay in a state of semi-coma unable to move or speak but conscious of what went on around him. Repeated requests to Noguchi to have him removed to the Bangkok European Hospital met with a blank refusal; meanwhile, the boy was slowly dying. A valiant attempt had been made to remove the tumour in the camp he had previously been in. A saw was made out of a piece of wire, with which a British surgeon cut through the skull and removed part of the tumour. The operation relieved the pressure, allowed the tumour to expand outside the skull and so prolonged his life; the one hope then was that we might be freed in time for medical skill to carry the work further. The boy did in fact survive until the day of our release, when he was removed to Bangkok by train, flown to Rangoon and from there direct to America. I do not know the end of his story, but our own doctors were of the opinion that there was little hope.

Chapter 26

The Drower Incident

Some time in June 1945 there occurred an incident which infuriated us all beyond anything we had endured in this hateful camp.

A young officer of the name of Drower used to act as Japanese interpreter for Colonel Toosey, the British Camp Commandant, and one day an altercation arose concerning some of our officers using the water pump at a time when the Japanese NCOs wanted to use it. A Japanese sergeant called Shimojo, whom we all hated with particular venom, was the cause of the trouble. This man ordered all the officers who were drawing water at the time to stand to attention in the blazing sun, and kept them standing there for several hours.

Drower went along to the Japanese administration office and tried to intervene on their behalf. After considerable argument, the Japanese sergeant and his companions lost their tempers and one of them hit Drower on the face, as was their usual custom. Although we had learnt by years of bitter experience that no useful purpose was served by retaliating, on this occasion Drower was unable, or perhaps courageously unwilling, to accept the insult and hit back. The result was a free-for-all lasting several minutes, until he was overpowered by numbers and taken off to the guardroom, where he was quite unmercifully kicked and beaten unconscious, then thrown into an underground cell near the guard house. There he was left with no blankets, no medical attention and no food for the rest of that day. Toosey made every endeavour to persuade Noguchi, the despicable Japanese captain in charge of the camp, to let him out, but it was no use. The next day, he was given one meal of rice and water and left in darkness, and this treatment went on for days. Toosey repeatedly asked for his release, for more food and blankets and for our own doctor to be allowed to visit him, or failing that, for him to be removed to some less vile place of imprisonment; but every request was met with a flat refusal.

The only contact we had at all was when his food was taken to him by one of our own officers, and then no conversation was permitted. Day after day,

Toosey tried to obtain some easement of the punishment, but Noguchi and his staff refused to listen.

It was obvious that such a situation could not continue for long without having serious effects on Drower's health, and so the doctors supplied Vitamin B tablets to the cookhouse staff, who powdered them up and mixed them with his rice. It was little enough but all that could be done for the time being, and it was felt that if his strength could be sustained, there was hope that the day would come when Noguchi would release him and his life might be saved. What they could not combat was the dampness of his dungeon and the mental strain of solitary confinement in the dark.

Some two weeks went by and still the barbaric punishment continued. Then a further surge of 'hate' was vented upon the whole camp. We were confined to our huts for a fortnight. The only time we were allowed out of them was to visit the latrines and ablution benches, the latter twice a day. The cooks of course were permitted to go to the cookhouse, and mess orderlies could go and fetch our meals to the huts, but that was all. In their efforts to make our imprisonment more irksome, our captors forbade us to play cards or any games, or even to read before six o'clock in the evening, which allowed us two hours before we had to be in our beds (so called) with all lights extinguished and in silence.

The Japanese thought that this treatment would subdue us and break what they called our 'obstinate spirit', but in fact it had the opposite effect, and the more offensive they became, the more our spirits rose. Admittedly, we felt time hang even heavier than usual, with no occupations from morning till evening except that of eating our not very exciting meals; but after the first day or two we found ways of dissipating the hours of boredom and outwitted the Japs by posting our own sentries in every hut to warn us of their approach, while we gathered in small groups to listen to talks on every imaginable subject or play some card game, the evidence of which could be removed at a moment's notice. Reading a book was inadvisable because one was liable to become too deeply engrossed in it to hear the quiet but timely warning of our sentry.

The knowledge that the Japanese were aware they had failed in their intentions was a great moral tonic for us, and we began to feel we could cheerfully endure this situation indefinitely. They just couldn't understand our mentality. Our only serious concern was for poor Bill Drower, who was still incarcerated in his dungeon and for whom we could do nothing.

At the end of a fortnight the Japs summoned Phil Toosey and informed him gravely that they considered that we had learnt our lesson, that we would now no doubt be more obedient and that they would therefore allow us to resume our normal activities.

The talks during this restricted period given by people to small groups of perhaps a dozen or so about occupations, hobbies or experiences of interest in civil life or in other services before the war proved extremely popular, and we heard some most interesting stories and broadened our knowledge on a wide range of subjects. I gave quite a number myself on such subjects as cotton spinning, dairy farming and beekeeping. I was surprised by the interest aroused and still more so by the amount of knowledge I found I possessed on these subjects, particularly the last named, in which my experience was limited to about three years prior to the war. I can only hope that if any of my audience took up beekeeping after they got home, they did not rely entirely on what they learnt from me!

After we were let out again we continued the practice in other huts, and often in the evenings, when the sudden tropical darkness had fallen and our home-made lights composed of old tins filled with coconut oil and with bits of string for wicks proved insufficient for reading by, we used to sit around in groups in the huts or on the parade ground, listening to all kinds of interesting and amusing adventures from the long gone pre-war days of peace.

For some weeks there had been rumours of an impending move from Kanburi to the eastern part of Siam, where the Japanese evidently considered we should be less of an embarrassment in the event of an Allied invasion of Siam from the Burmese border. By one means and another, our Intelligence Service contrived to piece together a sketchy but remarkably accurate picture of the Allied advance in all theatres, so that we were fairly well assured that the tide had turned in our favour and there was a reasonable chance of our imprisonment ending in the not too distant future; it was therefore understandable that our captors should consider it desirable to move us farther away from what might become a battle area.

At the same time, we had an uncomfortable feeling that, given the slightest provocation, they would have no hesitation in liquidating us all if we exhibited too aggressive a spirit or caused them to think that we were in any way capable of being of military value to our own side. Subsequently it was proved that our deductions were correct; in fact we were told after our release that a date about the middle of September had been fixed for our mass execution.

In due course, Toosey was told to organize us into parties of four hundred which would leave at weekly intervals; there were to be eight parties and the first was to consist of the fittest men in the camp, as they would not only have to march many miles, carrying all their equipment, but would also be required to build the new camp when they arrived at their destination.

Tremendous preparations were made by those selected in organizing and compressing what few belongings we all now possessed into the smallest possible and most convenient compass for a long forced march. Packs and bundles were packed and re-packed; articles of lesser value to their owners reluctantly discarded one by one until each man had reduced his load to a size and weight he felt capable of carrying. Having done this, many people daily rehearsed the drill and walked for several hours up and down the camp road loaded with their kit, in order to make themselves as fit as possible before the great trek began.

With the exception of the first one, from which we were debarred, all lieutenant colonels were allowed to choose which party they preferred. In the light of our limited knowledge of events outside, I developed a 'hunch' that the war would end either in August or September with the Americans making an all-out attack on the Japanese mainland, or that it would continue until the spring, when climatic conditions would be more favourable for delivering the *coup de grâce*. With these thoughts in mind, it seemed politic to remain as long as possible where I was, in the faint hope that the first alternative might come to pass. The final party was obviously one to avoid, since those who went with it would no doubt have to carry, in addition to their own impedimenta, all the bits and pieces which the Japanese had omitted to take on the earlier parties. I therefore chose the next to last party.

One by one, they left at weekly intervals, travelling by train to Bangkok which necessitated de-training en route to cross a river where the railway bridge had been bombed, either in native boats or by walking along planks laid over the broken spans, and entraining again on the other side. From Bangkok, they made a further train journey and then a final march of some 50 or 60 miles to their final destination at Nakon Nayok. Toosey went with the first party and handed over our camp to Commander Alexander RN.

Word came back to us that they had had a pretty grim journey but had survived it and were now engaged in the construction of the new camp in a godforsaken bit of country miles from civilization.

All this time, poor Bill Drower was still imprisoned in his dark and filthy dugout and was reported to be very weak, suffering repeated attacks of malaria and becoming mentally affected. By this time, certain of the Koreans who had always been relatively friendly began to show resentment against the treatment Noguchi had meted out to him; they had every cause to dislike Noguchi just as much as we did and they collaborated with us in smuggling in some blankets, quinine and a better allowance of more suitable food.

Noguchi was still with us, and we thought that he would be sure to release Drower when he (Noguchi) left for Nakon Nayok. But no, he gave his Adjutant strict orders that Drower was not to be released. When Noguchi eventually left Kanburi in his 15cwt truck, he took with him the much hated Sergeant Shimojo, for which we were profoundly thankful.

Quite unknown to him, he also took with him our wireless set, dismantled and the bits carefully secreted among the miscellaneous collection of camp utensils comprising the truck's load! This intrepid piece of daring was again performed by the brothers Max and Donald Webber, who accompanied his party and, at the other end of the journey, when the Japanese had finally capitulated, had the satisfaction of informing Noguchi of what they had done and of instructing him to obtain some batteries for them so that the set might again operate!

Noguchi left his Adjutant, Lieutenant Matsushita, in charge of those us who remained in Kanburi. Matsushita was really a very decent little man, who had always done his best to smooth things out for the prisoners wherever he had been, and he had many little acts of genuine kindness to his credit which would have meant great trouble for him from his superiors had they ever been discovered. This poor little man didn't dare let Drower out, but he at once allowed our doctors to visit him and do what they could under the circumstances. They reported that he was in a shocking and extremely weak state, and that his mind was seriously deranged.

Days went by, and July gave place to August. The weekly parties continued to leave for the new camp until there were only some eight hundred of us left behind. The following week, my party would go, and we started the routine of packing and unpacking, discarding this and that because it was too heavy or too bulky; donning our best set of shorts and shirts, boots and socks – all kept in reserve and not normally worn in camp so as to be ready for such an occasion or even for the happier one which we knew would one day come when we might be free men once more; and taking our daily walk fully loaded up and down the camp to make ourselves as fit as possible for the journey.

Chapter 27

A New Dawn Breaks

One morning, we paraded as usual for the daily *tenko* (the Japanese for roll call). The Japanese officers and sergeants came on parade, trailing their long swords, clearing their throats and spitting as they walked, but without the usual arrogance and swagger.

From our silent ranks there came a subdued murmur of surprised comment. Everyone noticed the difference at once: their faces looked pale and anxious and had taken on a dirty, sickly colour. Something had happened which had shaken them badly; excitement became intense. Roll call was taken quickly, then we were summarily dismissed and a perfect buzz of excitement broke out; speculation ran to the dizziest heights – what could have happened?

During the morning, a party of officers were taken out of camp to the railway to unload stores and two of them came back with a very strange story. They said that as they approached the station, a Thai came along on a bicycle and, as he got level with them, he dismounted and whispered the word 'Peace', then got on his bicycle and rode off.

We were very puzzled by this account, because although several of us were acquainted with a number of the Siamese inhabitants of Kanburi and the locality, we knew none who we thought possessed enough English to know the word; we doubted if even our old friend Boon Pong would know it, although the description the officers brought back seemed to fit him.

The Intelligence Centre set all its spies to work throughout the camp, and the next bit of information came from one of the few Other Ranks in the camp. This man was a tailor by trade and worked in the Japanese part of the camp mending Japanese and Korean uniforms, not of his own choice, but by order of the Japs. A Korean had come in with some piece of clothing to be mended and, as usual, started to talk in broken English, coming out with the statements, 'Oru (all) men go home. War all finish. Big bomb fall. Many, many Jappons paradiso!'

This brief but informative titbit was taken hot foot to the Intelligence Centre; things were beginning to fit together. Somebody caught a glimpse of a small Union Jack being waved from the window of a Siamese house in the town, and excitement became intense. What could it all mean? Had the Americans landed in Japan? Had the US Pacific Fleet (which the Japs had many times tried to persuade us was at the bottom of the sea) at last cornered and wiped out the Japanese fleet?

Our spirits and our excitement rose higher and higher as the day wore on. Several of our officers who worked in our Headquarters Administration office spoke fluent Japanese and they concentrated their efforts on the very unpleasant Japanese interpreter. At last, during the afternoon, they succeeded in extracting from him the tremendous news of the Hiroshima atomic bomb and subsequent order to capitulate issued by the Emperor.

As the news spread round the camp, we all went wild with excitement. Commander Alexander took one of our Japanese-speaking officers to Matsushita's office and told him that we knew what had happened and that we were therefore no longer prisoners.

Everybody collected on the broad road through the camp up and down which most of us had walked so many miles in the last six months, while miraculously a Union Jack, the Stars and Stripes and the Dutch flag were produced from heaven knows where and nailed to three bamboo poles lashed to the gable ends of the three centre huts in the long line. As the Union Jack fluttered from its improvised flagpole, the voices of some four hundred British swelled into the national anthem, and never have I heard it sung with deeper feeling or more emotion. Then all the British officers stood at attention while the Dutch sang their anthem with equal fervour.

The relief was almost overwhelming after three and a half years of perpetual mental strain and anxiety; we felt that a great load had been suddenly lifted off our shoulders, and in that moment we were the happiest people on earth. The fact that we were in rags, that we might have to go on eating rice and only rice for many more meals, that release from this hateful camp might be a long time in coming, counted for nothing. The one thought uppermost in all our minds was that we had managed to live through this long drawn out period of nightmare existence and that at last the dawn of our freedom was brightening before us.

The first surge of delirious excitement was followed by a feeling of peaceful relief, quiet, triumphant happiness and thankfulness to God. He had seen fit to watch over us in our adversity and to lead us through the darkness of our existence into the light of peace and freedom once more.

Commander Alexander now formed a kind of Executive Committee of senior officers to tackle the many problems which immediately arose and to determine our next moves.

Immediately the truth of the Japanese capitulation was made known to us, the first person to be thought of was of course poor Bill Drower, who for all these weeks had lain sick and uncared for in the vile dugout near the guardroom. He was in a bad way, and we removed him at once to a vacated Japanese hut, where our doctors and hospital orderlies could give him the best available medical skill and nursing. Repeated attacks of malaria, damp and filthy surroundings, darkness and insufficient food with inadequate vitamin content had played havoc with him and had affected his mind as well as his body.

He had been allowed neither to wash nor to shave and was in a pitiable condition when rescued. For several days he was carefully nursed in our camp and then, as signs of improvement became discernible, he was taken to another camp where there was a slightly better equipped hospital and a larger medical staff; there he gradually improved, until he was sufficiently strong to endure the journey by train to Bangkok and thence by air to Rangoon. I regret that I lost touch with his progress after leaving Tamuan, the hospital to which he went first from Kanburi, but I trust that his gallant spirit enabled him to make a complete recovery in the course of time. Shortly after the capitulation – by way of adding insult to injury – the Japanese general who had been in charge of all PoWs and who had known all about him all the time, had the audacity to send him a letter expressing regret at the treatment he had received and a case of inferior champagne!

The next thing we did was to hold a service of thanksgiving for all denominations in the camp, and I should doubt if there was a single absentee. We also told Matsushita that since we were no longer prisoners we proposed to go out of the camp as we wished. As he had received no orders from his superiors, this caused him a big headache. In order to ease matters a little for him, we said we would be content for the first evening with a walk out on to the open ground outside the camp between us and the town, where we would play a game of football in order to demonstrate our peaceful intentions to all and sundry; but we would not go into town, where we should no doubt meet many Japanese soldiers who might create trouble.

Of course, as soon as we appeared on the old airfield that evening, almost the entire population swarmed across from the town, patting us on the back, laughing, shaking hands with us, showering cakes and fruit upon us and pressing packets of cigarettes into our hands.

A number of us had learnt sufficient Siamese to understand and make ourselves intelligible, and we were able to tell them that we would come into the town the next evening, whereupon many invitations were pressed upon us to visit homes.

Next morning, we sent out a small deputation to visit our old friend Boon Pong, who owned the most prosperous general store in Kanburi. In the party was Keith Bostock, an Australian Red Cross representative, who pledged his government's credit for a large sum and arranged with Boon Pong for deliveries of much needed food supplies, which duly arrived in a broken-down old motor lorry with flat tyres held on to the wheels with bits of wire and rope. It was laden high with chickens, eggs, bananas, fruit of all kinds, vegetables and a hundred other useful and pleasing cooking accessories, and thereafter our meals become veritable feasts. He also unearthed his big wireless, which had been concealed from the Japanese for so long – the Siamese not being permitted to have wireless sets either – and set it up in his shop. We arranged a constant relay of people to listen to the programmes from Allied sources and to take down the news bulletins, which were then posted up in the camp.

Everybody made expeditions to the town and bought razor blades, soap, toothpaste and brushes, in fact everything essential of which we had been so long in need, while at every turn hospitality was showered upon us by the friendly Thais. In some houses they also produced bottles of the exceedingly potent local 'hooch' called *laow*, made from rice. In their hospitality they pressed it upon us so freely that there were unfortunate results in some cases. Deprived of anything of the sort for so long, it proved too much for some of our number in their reduced condition. However, the victims were assisted or carried back to camp, and there were no 'incidents'.

The town was full of disgruntled and surly looking Japanese soldiers, of whom the Thais now openly showed their dislike and of whom we took no notice. Our own former guards did not interfere in any way with our comings and goings, and a day or two later, Alexander ordered Matsushita to parade his men and hand over all their arms, which they obediently did. We then moved them into a considerably more circumscribed area of the camp and assumed command ourselves, mounting our own guard – unarmed – on the camp entrance.

By this time, we had re-established contact with the last party that had left for the new camp in eastern Siam. They had learnt of the Japanese capitulation while still at Bangkok and had remained there in some godowns on the riverside. We arranged to reinforce them with a party of senior officers, mostly regulars, who were to set up a British HQ in Bangkok for the purpose of getting in touch with the various PoW camps throughout Siam and also to liaise with the British forces who, we were informed by radio, would fly in to Bangkok. These officers duly proceeded by train.

In addition, small parties of officers went off to such camps as we knew of and could get to by road and rail where our troops were still being made to work for the Japanese, in order to organize matters for the betterment of their conditions. News of the Japanese capitulation had spread to most of the camps, but there were some, miles from civilization, which we could not contact, and in these, conditions of hardship and brutality continued, the Japanese being unaware or unwilling to believe that they had been defeated.

During the first week or two, several trainloads of sick men arrived at Kanburi from some of those camps; most of them were in an appalling state, quite as bad as anything we had seen during the worst period of the building of the railway, and many of those who were not too ill to talk gave us ghastly accounts of the cruelty and privations still continuing. The incredulity of those who were not too sick to notice the flags flying in the camp when they arrived was quite pathetic; at first, they seemed unable to believe that the war was over and that they were once again free to all intents and purposes, even though it might be some time before they could be got out of the camp.

Everything possible was done for them within the limited scope of our environment, but we did at least have a better selection of essential drugs which had been flown in and dropped by parachute with other supplies, and these, together with the new zest for life, worked wonders with the majority; though tragically there were some who were beyond the limit of human endurance and who, in the hour of their release from hell in earth, passed on to their rest.

Chapter 28

Rehabilitation

By this time we had the local Japanese soldiery, who had been our captors for so long, just where we wanted them. They gave us no trouble at all and saluted us in a servile fashion whenever we came across them. The only exception was Matsushita, the little Adjutant left in charge after Captain Noguchi departed to organize the intended new camp in eastern Siam. He had always been at pains to help us whenever there was trouble with the other Japs, so far as was possible, and all of us really quite liked him. Quite obviously he now felt his position keenly and behaved with dignity, and although he could not speak more than a few words of English he made it very clear that he was deeply ashamed of the doings of his countrymen.

One of the biggest surprises we had almost immediately after the Japanese surrender was when a young American officer, armed to the teeth, walked into camp apparently out of the blue! We were still more astonished when the young man told us that he and several other Americans had been dropped by parachute into the jungle about 35km away some six weeks previously and had established a camp where, completely unknown to the Japanese, they had been busily training about a thousand young Thais in the art of jungle warfare.

Apparently the Japanese had got wind of something of the sort going on, but had been completely unsuccessful in obtaining any definite information about it or knowledge of its location. This accounted to some extent for their unexpected confinement of us to our huts for a fortnight some weeks earlier, which I have already described. Our American friend told us that he had two-way wireless contact with SEAC [South East Asia Command] at Colombo and asked for a list of our most pressing needs, saying that he would request they be dropped by air immediately. He got a very comprehensive list forthwith!

After this he visited us daily and about two days later brought us instructions to prepare the open ground outside the camp for a parachute drop by Dakotas at 1800 hours that evening. Everyone was out on the site in an excited state well before the appointed time, and punctually at one minute to six we heard the well-known drone of planes coming in from the north. It was a wonderful sight to us and must have been an eye-opener for the Japanese and Siamese, who had never seen anything of the kind before. One after the other, six Dakotas roared low over the old landing ground, and as each passed over, from the open doors in their flanks out tumbled bale after bale of food, clothing and medical stores. Slowly the parachutes opened and soon the air was full of them falling gently to earth. Unfortunately, a few parachutes failed to open, and in these cases the bales hurtled to the ground with a crash, scattering tins of food all over the area.

It was a wonderful feeling to be able to wave to the crews in the planes as they circled round and round the camp and to feel that now we really were in direct contact with home. The whole town was there and watched in awed silence this demonstration of Allied efficiency and resource, while our former captors watched in equal astonishment and were obviously deeply impressed. When the last plane had zoomed over us – the crew waving gaily in response to our frenzied ovation from below – and had flown off in the direction of home, we fell upon the booty, removing load after load into the camp in two Japanese lorries which we had commandeered; whereupon all those who, before the days of captivity, had belonged to the 'Q' side of their units took charge, revelling in the unusual experience, no doubt, of re-issuing stores expendable and non-expendable, without signatures!

Within twenty-four hours we were all once more respectably clad and equipped with the main essentials of hygiene such as soap, toothpaste, razor blades, towels and the like; and were enjoying again British cigarettes and tobacco and tinned food of every description, pleasures practically unknown to us for more than three years. The moral effect of this was terrific, and we soon began to feel on top of the world again.

Within a day or so of this great event, M Salzmann, the Swiss Red Cross representative from Bangkok, came up to see us and spent the night in the camp. He told us that of course he knew all about us but had been powerless to do anything for us while the Japanese were in control of the country. He took a lot of photographs of the camp, many of which have been reproduced since for the Far East PoW Association. I asked him if he would like to accompany me to Chungkai to see what was left of the camp and to try and recover my diary and other papers which, as I have mentioned earlier, I had buried in the cemetery.

Armed with a spade and a compass, we crossed the Quaiyai river at Kanburi in a native canoe paddled by two small but skilful Thai children and walked along the riverside path which I had traversed many times before, but then accompanied by a Korean guard. We walked past the scattered Thai and Chinese huts with their vegetables gardens, passing the time of day cheerily with the inhabitants, most of whom knew me by sight and all of whom made it perfectly plain that they were delighted by the change in their situation and overjoyed at the downfall of Japan.

After about a mile and a half we arrived at the cemetery, where we were pleased to find that although vegetation was springing up everywhere, it was quite easy to find the grave in which I had buried my papers. While I was digging, M Salzmann took a number of photos of the cemetery and a most unprepossessing one of me in the rather ghoulish task on which I was engaged, and these he sent to me after I returned home.

I recovered the treasure and carefully tidied up the grave again, then we went on to have a look at the site of the old camp, where so much had happened in the preceding years. We found that on evacuating it the Japanese had pulled down and burnt all the former huts, and although it was barely four months ago, the tropical vegetation had sprung up so fast that I found it quite difficult to locate the position of my old camp HQ in which I had lived for many months.

By now – six years later – no doubt not a sign remains of that small area in which, during the period of its existence, some 30,000 men spent some part of their days of captivity and in which 1,500 of them died. Only the cemetery remains, as a lasting memorial to those who were unable to stand up to the years of inhuman treatment meted out to them by their vicious and despicable captors.

Time may dim the feelings and obliterate the memories of those who have read or heard the story, but in the heart of every ex-PoW who passed through the Siamese prison camps will remain a deep-rooted and eternal hatred and scorn and a memory of starvation, brutality and depravity far beyond comprehension of any but those who were the victims of the Japanese and their Korean guards.

Chapter 29

Freedom at Last

At about four o'clock on the morning of 25 August 1945, I was rudely awakened by someone seizing me by one foot in the dark and saying, 'Do you want to go home?'

Only half awake, but sufficiently in command of my senses to know where I was, what an inane question it seemed. 'Don't be a BF,' I replied politely and turned over to go to sleep again.

'Do you want to go home? Because if you do, you've got to leave here in an hour,' came the voice again out of the darkness.

By this time, I was wide enough awake to realize that there was a general commotion throughout the length of the long hut, and oil lamps began to splutter into life here and there. My informant told me that a train was to leave for Bangkok in an hour's time and that if I wanted to go on it I had better get a move on.

This was a new and wonderful thought, but I knew that there were many men of my regiment in various camps up and down Siam and I wanted to make sure that they were also being sent home, so it needed little consideration for me to decide to remain where I was for the time being.

Further sleep was now out of the question in the pandemonium that was raging in the hut, so those who had decided to stay behind got dressed and we all helped to carry baggage to the train and saw our friends off on the first stage of their journey to freedom, entrusting them with cables to send off at the first possible moment to our relatives at home.

When daylight came, we surveyed the turmoil of our usually tidy hut. Everything except essentials had been discarded in the exodus, and the litter was indescribable. We spent most of that day making bonfires and tidying up the place. There were then only about a hundred of us left, and we spent a peaceful, uneventful and even quite pleasant existence for the next few days, coming and going as we pleased and visiting other camps in the neighbourhood by motor truck to see how their respective troops were faring; we were glad to find the same procedure happening, with parties leaving every day or two for Bangkok.

On 5 September we were told that there would be another train by which we could travel; so having assured myself that all the men of my own regiment who I had been able to contact either had already gone or were on the point of doing so, I packed my few belongings and went too. It was a slow journey and we took all day to do about 70 miles. At one point, our planes had bombed the bridge over a river, and we all had to de-train, load our baggage into boats and send it across, then do a hair-raising tightrope act along crazy planks laid across the twisted girders of the bridge some 40ft above the water. Arriving on the other side, we sat for about two hours in the blazing sun on the railway line until a train arrived to take us on our way.

Eventually, we arrived at the riverside in Bangkok just after dark and were directed into motor boats, which ferried us across to a landing stage, where we were met by some of our own people who directed us to various billets in schools and public buildings, where we were housed for the next few days. My birthday occurred during these few days, and I celebrated the event by taking a couple of friends to have a very indifferent meal at what had formerly been a large European-style hotel, after which we walked through the city and came upon an open-air cafe where the local inhabitants continued to dance far into the night; we were interested spectators but did not participate.

A considerable amount of British War Department transport had been recaptured from the Japanese, and by means of this we were able to see quite a lot of the city while we were waiting for air transport to take us to Rangoon. Among other places, we visited the Royal Buddhist temple and several other temples near to it. They were really most interesting and full of weird and wonderful carved ornaments, Buddhas and painted murals. The city is an unbelievable mixture of modern Western architecture and town planning and primitive Oriental squalor. Imposing stone and concrete buildings set among wide tree-lined avenues create an atmosphere of dignity and culture as one drives through the city, only for it to be rudely shattered a moment later by the sight of tin-roofed shanties, bamboo and *attap* palm huts and the usual squalor and smell of the native quarters of most Asian towns and villages.

Some of the shops were quite well stocked with the products of Japan – the only source of supply – but all very expensive owing to the inflation of the Siamese currency.

There were a number of jewellers' shops, where one could buy very attractive ornaments, cigarette cases and jewellery made of the local silver and set with the semi-precious stones of the country. I think most of us came home with a selection of these for our families. Unfortunately, at this early stage of our return we were not over-endowed with the necessary cash, and our purchases were more limited than they otherwise might have been.

On the morning of 10 September my party was ordered to be at the aerodrome by 11 o'clock. On the way there I called at the British HQ which had been set up by the incoming Indian Division in conjunction with some of our senior British ex-PoW officers – mostly regulars – who had gone there immediately the Japanese capitulated, to set up a communication centre. As I was leaving the building, I met Osata, who had been Commandant of Chungkai camp during my first year and with whom I had always got on amicably. In those days, although he was only a lieutenant, I always had to salute him. Now, however, I received a very smart salute. He was the last Japanese I was to encounter. Had all the Japanese officers been men of his mentality and calibre, our troubles would have been far fewer.

On arrival at the aerodrome, my party embarked in three Dakotas, about 30 men to each machine. We were soon off and we asked the pilot of our plane if he would take us over the camp at Kanburi so that we could drop some mail and small parcels for our friends who had remained behind to wind the camp up. Soon we were over the camp, and the pilot circled low over the open ground outside it while we waved to the small figures below us and threw our parcels out through the door in the side with little parachutes attached to them.

Still waving as we circled once more, gaining height, we headed away north, climbing above the endless green jungle, leaving behind us at last those years of purgatory interspersed alternatively with hope, disillusion, despair, hope again, and now the fulfilment of our dreams.

Up and ever up, until the miles of jungle lay like a green carpet below us streaked with silver threads where the blazing sun glinted on the rivers; up through the clouds until we came to a realm where we floated in space with only the sun above and a fleecy white carpet of cloud below.

At last our troubles were ended and happiness and home lay ahead.

Never again would the hated cry of '*Koorah*' sound in our ears.

Family Epilogue

We two sisters, Pat Davies and Jean Argles, remember our pre-war childhood as a time of secure routine – lessons with governesses shared with our younger brother Robert, rides on our pony Dolly, family summer weekend tennis parties and winter shoots, fishing holidays in Scotland and church on Sundays: our parents' strong Christian faith would help to sustain each of them later. We lived with our father's father, a widower, in his Lancashire country house, and every weekday morning he and our father went off to the cotton-spinning mill which, with the rents from tenant farms on the estate, provided the family income.

We admired our father greatly for a number of reasons. He was tall and handsome, he could solve any problem, he enjoyed jokes and he had a lovely tenor singing voice. Jean remembers coming down the stairs listening to him sing and accompanying himself on the piano long before she could understand the words. After tea we used to stand round the piano singing sea shanties with him, piping away at 'What Shall We Do with a Drunken Sailor?' and 'Boney Was a Warrior'. He was the leading actor in local productions of *The Desert Song* and *Rose Marie*, and he rode his horse Sandy in a Lancaster pageant as Bonnie Prince Charlie.

Our father was always very interested in, and concerned by, anything which affected the people whose lives crossed with his own. In the family cotton-spinning mills he knew all the workers, including their children and families, by name and was much more concerned for their welfare than he was for his own when the industry collapsed in later years. This of course came out clearly in his concern for the soldiers under his command, as the letters to our mother from relatives and survivors confirmed, and also, in his later days, for the families on the farms and in our local village.

Our father was just old enough to have served in the Royal Marines towards the end of the First World War, and he followed this up by joining the Territorial Army, going off to camp every summer. So of course in

August 1939, with war threatening, we cut short a Scottish camping holiday to rush back for him to rejoin his regiment, the 137th Field Regiment, Royal Artillery, in Blackpool.

During the first months of the war our family life was not too seriously disrupted. With the regiment training in South Lancashire and Cheshire he could come home on weekend leave, or invite us over for family visits. It was only when they moved to Larkhill on Salisbury Plain for further training that he and our mother were really separated for the first time in twenty years. Pat was in her first job, in London, filling in time until she could join the women's services, and on visits to Larkhill she realized how much he was enjoying life in the army, and how popular and respected he was.

We were all at home for his embarkation leave in September 1941, Jean and Bob on holiday from their Warwickshire boarding schools. We fished a local lake – 'Daddy got six very nice trout on dry fly', Pat's diary recorded. But the family mood puzzled her: 'Everyone rather remarkably cheerful, thought we might well have been somewhat depressed. It's worst for poor Mama and Bob, of course.' No doubt we were reflecting our father's exhilaration at the prospect of action after two years of training. Our grandfather opened a bottle of the '96 port; and the next morning our father left.

When our father disappeared from the lives of our close affectionate family, we were teenagers and Bob was eleven. For over three years we and our mother did not know if we should ever see him again. The grim tension of those years was to end with the joy of his return. Our family was lucky, as so many were not.

During his voyage in *Dominion Monarch* our mother wrote to him almost every day, as he did to her. They had agreed to number their letters, and he would use friends' names as private code to tell her where he was going. 'Kathleen Jenkins' would mean Singapore. His letters reached her, after some delay. Every one of hers to him, addressed c/o Army Post Office 1310, would eventually be returned stamped 'Addressee Reported Missing' – none of the news from home he was longing to receive ever reached him. During his passage out the Japanese entered the war, but all the same the atmosphere at Christmas 1941 was fairly optimistic. We missed him intensely; but his presents of stockings for us and books for Bob which he posted in Cape Town duly arrived. The next news was his cable to say they had landed in Singapore.

Reports came that the Malayan campaign was going badly, and in mid-February Singapore fell – an immense shock. The following weeks were a time of great tension. All our men were reported 'Missing', so families did not know if they had survived the campaign, until at last in April the Japanese issued lists of prisoners. Our mother put a notice of his survival in national and local newspapers. Families and friends exchanged any scrap of information. Not until the autumn did his first format postcard arrive, and, as these cards were reported to have been delayed by some months, we only knew that he had been alive at some earlier time. Atrocity stories of the Japanese treatment of prisoners filled the newspapers, horrific reading for relatives.

Our mother carried on running the household with our grandfather. Pat was at home at this time and remembers how her mother made the school holidays as normal as she could for Jean and Bob, keeping them informed in termtime of any news. She served as an Air Raid Precautions warden; and when her father was bombed out of his retirement hotel in Bath he joined our household. Throughout the war our mother's courage was admirable.

Country life in wartime, with no entertainments and little petrol, was desperately boring for teenagers. Each of us sisters made our evenings when we were at home more interesting by chatting with our grandfather's Austrian refugee cook, and so acquired fairly fluent conversational German. From August 1942 Pat was able to use this as a Special Duties Linguist in the Women's Royal Naval Service (the Wrens), intercepting German naval Enigma Code messages at Bletchley Park's secret coastal 'Y' radio out-stations, while on her eighteenth birthday in November 1943 Jean joined the First Aid Nursing Yeomanry (the FANYs), and after training with Special Operations Executive (S.O.E.) in Baker Street, spent the next two years as a code and cipher operator in Egypt and Italy. We each signed the Official Secrets Act, and it was years after the war before we told each other or anyone else what our secret war work had been. Always in our minds was the tension and anxiety of not knowing what was happening to our father, always being prepared for bad news. Like everyone else we joined in the celebration of victory in Europe in May 1945; but for families like ours by far the most important day was VJ Day in August. Soon after, his cable arrived from Rangoon, saying that he was on his way home.

The War Office wisely brought prisoners of war from the Far East the slow way home by sea, to feed them up, relax, and catch up on what had been happening in their absence before they met their families again. Later on, our father would tell Jean that he talked to his men, explaining that their wives and families wouldn't know what had been happening to them, might think that they had had an easier time than people left at home to cope with air raids and rationing, and that they must be patient and understanding. He also managed to bring us all small presents from Thailand, just as if he had been on holiday.

When he finally arrived back in England it was inevitably a tense moment for us all. Jean remembers being very nervous as we waited in the drawing room, wondering if he would look very different and how he would be feeling about us who had not suffered as he had done, which we now knew more about. In fact, he looked very much as we remembered, though of course much thinner. As he was accompanied by a civic official who had clearly had a few drinks on the way – probably from nervousness about his task – our long-awaited family reunion was nearer comedy than drama.

He had a long spell of paid leave to begin with, as was normal for returning prisoners, and spent much of it getting the very overgrown garden back into shape and fitting in visits to relations and friends. Inevitably, universities, post-war jobs – some of which took us abroad – and in due course our marriages meant that, although we always kept in touch, we were not able to spend very much time with our parents in the years after the war. When we did, we were much impressed by the many responsibilities he was soon taking on. He was asked to form and command a new TA regiment, 337 HAA, at Blackpool, then became honorary colonel of 288 Air Defence Regiment, TA. He joined our grandfather as a magistrate, succeeded him as a Chairman of the family firm, and was awarded an OBE for services to the cotton industry, in a difficult time when government policy to locate spinning exclusively to India meant many Lancashire mills – including ours – eventually closing down. He was Chairman and President of the Royal Lancashire Agricultural Society, Chairman of Lunesdale Farmers, and in 1965 he was High Sheriff of Lancashire.

Our father had to cope with the situation of coming home to a household where his octogenarian father understandably wanted to retain his role as head of the family, sitting at the top of the table for all meals, employing all indoor and outdoor staff and generally running our domestic lives as he had done throughout much of the war. This continued until our grandfather's very old age, when he was confined to a wheelchair and needed constant care but was still very aware of everything that went on around him. It could not help but be a painful situation at times for both men. Our father coped with it amazingly patiently.

He kept in touch with other ex-prisoners and went to reunions of the Far East Prisoners of War Association in London; but at home he talked very little about his life in the camps. He had a lifelong hatred of anything Japanese. He did not tell us that he had been physically ill-treated, although other prisoners had given witness of this and of his courage, as Mr A. B. Miller does in a letter to the *Lancaster Guardian* printed at the end of this book. He found time to do some editing of the secret diary he had kept in little notebooks and hidden first in bamboo poles and finally in a bottle in a grave in Chungkai Cemetery – the text of this book. Later he gave the diary itself to the Imperial War Museum in London.

When Pat's job as a television producer involved filming in Thailand, in the 1960s, our father wrote to Boon Pong, the Thai merchant who had taken great risks to supply the Allied prisoners with medicines and wireless batteries, and she spent a day with him by the River Kwai. 'Boon Pong pointed out sites of camps along the road,' she wrote home, 'but all that remained was some of the earth bank along the perimeter – the jungle has grown all over them . . . the cemetery at Kanchenburi is most beautifully and tidily kept, with rose bushes between the graves . . . the one at Chungkai has a large stone just inside the gate with the inscription "Their Name Liveth for Evermore" on it. It is even more remote and peaceful, and the birds sing just like in England in spring.'

Chungkai camp was also completely overgrown, but the railway line was intact and in use. Back in his house, Boon Pong pointed to his chair and said, 'Your father have lunch here day after war ended. I invite him.' He gave Pat a present of Thai silk and sent a silver dollar to our father. Her letter ended: 'Chungkai is a lovely place – all that misery and violence would seem almost unbelievable but for the evidence of the railway and cemeteries; the peace of the countryside seems to have flooded back.'

We celebrated our parents' diamond wedding in 1982; but our mother's health was failing and she died in 1989. Jean lived near enough to spend time with the family whenever she could, and Bob, who had made his career in Africa, came back with his wife Anne for six years and looked after our mother with great care. But they had already decided that their retirement would be in Africa, where their children were, and not in Lancashire. Our father was desperately lonely without our mother. After Bob and Anne had left, he married a much younger second wife, Mrs Sarah Young, and when he died at home of cancer two years later, the house and estate were sold.

Another rather surprising talent that he had Jean only found when she was going through some old papers after he died (but one known to our mother since before they were married), was writing poetry – often light-heartedly, but sometimes with much deeper feeling.

A day or so before he died he asked Jean to drive him up to the moors behind the house, where at his request she left him to sit alone in the car and drink in the beauty of the hills around, which he loved so much – both in North Lancashire and in Scotland, walking, shooting, and fishing – all his life.

Our father had very much wanted his diary to be published, both as a record of what happened in the camps and to commemorate the many Allied soldiers who died there. It wasn't published in his lifetime, and we are so glad that it is being now. We are specially grateful to Henry Wilson of Pen & Sword for his helpful guidance to us in our writing of this family memoir, and to the staff of Pen & Sword including George Chamier, our copy editor.

We remember our father with great respect and admiration, as well as with much love and gratitude.

Pat Davies
Jean Argles
2016

Appendix

This letter was sent to the *Lancaster Guardian* on 15 January 1993.

Dear Sir,

May I, as an ex-Japanese Prisoner of War, through the courtesy of your columns, pay tribute to the memory of a fine and gallant Englishman.

Colonel Cary Owtram of Newland Hall, Lancaster was the Senior British Officer in charge of No.2 Group of Japanese prisoners employed on the construction of the notorious Burma/Siam railway.

On many occasions I witnessed his receiving brutal beatings for his adamant and steadfast refusals to order sick men out to work on the railway. This occurred on so many occasions that eventually even the Japanese accepted the fact that if Cary Owtram said so, then those men were indeed too sick to work.

There are many ex-PoWs, including myself, who owe their survival to Colonel Owtram.

Of the many so called 'camps' that existed up and down the railway the name of 'Chung-Kai' of which Cary Owtram was in charge, will be forever remembered by the thousands of Japanese prisoners who passed through it.

One of my own vivid personal memories was of one evening upon returning to Chung-Kai after an exhausting day on the railway, and joining hundreds of others enjoying a 'impromptu' concert, the 'star item' being Cary Owtram, with his beautiful tenor voice, dressed as the 'Red Shadow' singing excerpts from The Desert Song.

It is good to know that after those dark days of hunger, deprivation and brutality he survived to enjoy many happy years at his home at Newland and to die peacefully at the grand age of 93.

A. B. Miller